the Backcountry

Steve Edwards

UNIVERSITY OF NEBRASKA PRESS | LINCOLN AND LONDON

Library of Congress Cataloging-
in-Publication Data
Edwards, Steve, 1974–
Breaking into the backcountry /
Steve Edwards.
p.   cm.
ISBN 978-0-8032-2653-1
(cloth : alk. paper)
1. Edwards, Steve, 1974– 2. Authors,
American—21st century—Biography.
3. Outdoor life—Oregon. 4. Oregon—
Description and travel. I. Title.
PS3605.D89855Z46   2010
818'.6—dc22
[B]
2010002939

Set in Janson by Bob Reitz.
Designed by Nathan Putens.

Contents

Acknowledgments

I AM INCREDIBLY INDEBTED TO PEN/Northwest and the Boyden family, who made it possible for me to live and write at Dutch Henry Homestead as part of the PEN/Northwest Margery Davis Boyden Wilderness Writing Residency. The last thing I expected out of an excursion into solitude was to make new friends, but that's exactly what happened. For their kindness, generosity, and encouragement during my residency and beyond, I am thankful to John Daniel, Joe Green, Marquita Green, Frank Boyden, Ian Boyden, Jenny Boyden, and Dave Reed. And I owe a special thanks to Bradley Boyden—friend, mentor, force of nature—who shared with me his love and enthusiasm for all things Dutch Henry. For marathon fishing trips, whiskey on ice under the stars, more stories than I can hope to remember, and every other form of good action: thank you, Bradley.

For being there to answer the phone when I called, and for listening to my stories, I am grateful to my friends and family: Bill and Nancy Edwards, Mike and Jill Edwards, Maurice Metten, Aaron Miller, and Michelle Miller. For their friendship and inspiration along the writer's path, and for saving the letters I sent them, I am grateful to Patricia Henley and Kip Robisch.

For reading early drafts of my manuscript, I owe a tremendous debt of gratitude to my friends John Watson and Maura Giles-Watson.

For the University of Nebraska Press, and in particular Rob Taylor, I am grateful for all the time, care, and dedication you gave to my manuscript. Also, a very special thanks to Jonis Agee who convinced me to give nonfiction a shot, and to Tom Gannon for his encouragement.

Last and most especially I am grateful to my wife, Rebecca Bednarz, for all the love and support she gave me during the writing of this book.

Acknowledgments

BREAKING INTO
THE BACKCOUNTRY

PROLOGUE

January 2001

THE CALL CAME FROM JOHN DANIEL, the contest's coordinator: I had somehow managed to win the PEN/Northwest Margery Davis Boyden Wilderness Writing Residency, whose prize was a small cash stipend and seven months as caretaker of a backcountry homestead in what John called "unparalleled solitude" along the federally designated Wild and Scenic Rogue River in southwestern Oregon. Thrilled by some validation for my writing, I didn't give much thought to what living in unparalleled solitude might mean or what I would have to leave behind. Honestly, I was just happy to have won something. That was last May. Now that the calendar year has turned a page and I'm only a few months from finally lighting out, some apprehension is setting in.

I'm from Indiana, born and raised. Indiana is the only life I've ever known. Aside from all the fishing trips my father took my brother and me on as kids, I've never been much of an out-doorsman. I've done typical midwestern things like chopping and stacking firewood, mowing grass, raking leaves, detasseling corn. And I've always loved the woods, its quiet and birdsong, the way sunlight filters through green maple leaves. But I know nothing of wilderness. The word itself calls forth such seemingly contradictory ideas. On one hand wilderness means a place of natural beauty and peace. On the other hand wilderness means a place of deprivation and danger. The wilderness is where people get lost and die. The wilderness is where people go to find them-selves and be reborn. "There is an almost visible line," writes poet Gary Snyder, "that a person . . . [can] walk across: out of history and into a perpetual present, a way of life attuned to the slower and steadier processes of nature." And this is maybe what concerns me most these days—the thought of what it takes to swallow hard and cross that line.

During my mandatory visit to the homestead last summer, an overnight stay (the homestead's owners like to make sure their caretakers know exactly what they're getting themselves into), I saw a bear in a meadow. Since then I've been dreaming of bears, and the bears of my dreams have been killing me.

In one dream my mother has been to visit, and I'm going around closing doors and windows because a cold draft is blowing in. Before I can shut the last door, my mother's dog, Daisy—an old tan-coated retriever mutt—goes racing outside after a rabbit. I chase after her, and when I round the corner I'm taken aback: the dog is gone, and standing in her place is a strange tin-roofed structure, a kind of altar supported by four wooden posts, under which is an enormous black bear. The bear is sniffing the grass, taking a few tufts into its mouth. I realize that the bear hasn't seen or smelled me and for a moment feel incredibly lucky for this glimpse of such a beautiful animal. Then out of the corner of my eye I see a dark blur. It's another big bear, and it's charging me. I feel its paws on my chest and neck, its great heft knocking me to the ground.

Though scary, the dreams add some excitement to a life that for me, at twenty-six, still living in the town where I was born, has begun to feel ordinary. Not terrible. Just sort of *ordinary*. I teach my first-year writing classes at Purdue, hang out with friends and family, check e-mail, pay bills. Once a week I drive to the veterans' home, where I am a volunteer. I talk with a disabled World War II vet named Rocky, a former bantamweight boxer in the navy who has a notebook full of poems he'd like Willie Nelson to make into songs, and I talk to Gene, a Korean War vet who is in physical therapy to learn how to use a new prosthetic leg. He tells me, every time, that he can't wait to go bowling. "I'm gonna bowl me a strike!" Gene says, sweeping his arm.

One day as we're talking I tell Gene I'm going to Oregon in the spring and that I'm worried about bears. "Don't take no shit from no bear!" Gene says. "Get a shotgun. Or a handgun. Or a bow and arrow!"

For more practical advice I have a manual that Bradley, one of the homestead's owners, sent me. It's complete with hand-drawn maps, descriptions of the water system and the cabin, the typical flora and fauna to be found along the Rogue, a bird list a former resident put together, who to call in case of fire, and the chores I'll need to complete. The agreement on chores is that in exchange for seven months at the cabin I'll do the equivalent of an hour a day of routine caretaking.

To get myself ready for all this—to clear my head of anxiety—I like to take long walks in a little park near the village of Battle Ground. It was here in 1811 that the Battle of Tippecanoe took place and Tecumseh's dream of an Indian confederacy was lost. There is an obelisk for the dead U.S. soldiers, a statue of

William Henry Harrison, a dozen acres of old oak trees. Across the highway is Prophet's Rock, a rock outcropping where Chief Tecumseh's brother Tenskwatawa, the Prophet, sang to his warriors and sprinkled them with a potion he said would make them invincible. I like to climb to the top of this rock and look out over the highway and across a field of stubble corn, some railroad tracks in the distance. It is bitter cold in January, but I come here anyway because it's the only place nearby that somehow approximates the quiet and solitude in store for me in the Oregon backcountry. On one such visit to the rock and its surrounding patch of woods, walking as mindfully as I can, I see from a distance four white-tailed deer munching frozen acorns under an enormous oak. They are velvety, gorgeous. I try to move closer, but they see me and retreat out of sight down a draw. Because I don't want to scare them toward the highway, I change direction and come at them from the east. Maybe they hear me or have caught my scent on the breeze. Maybe their flight instinct has kicked in. Next I see them from the top of a hill, they are running straight at me. Four full-grown white-taileds. They thunder by within feet of me. So close I can feel the sharp thump of their hooves hitting the ground, that vibration, in my chest. It is perhaps one of the most amazing things I've ever seen or felt, and, afterward, standing there with a racing heart, I only wish that someone else had seen it, too. That I could have shared it.

Returning to my pickup later that morning, I get the chance. A cop has backed himself into the little gravel parking lot to clock speeders. He's got a Styrofoam cup of coffee in one hand, a radar gun in the other. "Just saw four deer up there," I'll say to him, thumbing at the woods behind me. "Ran right past me," I'll say. "Close enough I could've reached right out and touched them."

I imagine the story might somehow redeem what for the cop, out here in the cold, clocking speeders on a nearly empty highway, is an otherwise ordinary, boring morning. If he likes the story and we get to talking, maybe I'll tell him about my trip to Oregon. It's the kind of thing people like to hear about—someone stepping onto a ledge. But as I head back to my pickup, ready with what I'll say, I start to wonder: What would it feel like if I *didn't* tell the cop about the deer I saw? What if I didn't tell anyone? How would it feel to walk around with the glimmer of that little story inside me like a secret? And so in the end, rather than pausing to chat, I walk right past the cop. I climb into my pickup and drive away.

GETTING THERE

BY MIDAFTERNOON WE'VE CROSSED IOWA ON I-80 and started north to South Dakota on I-29. It's the same route we took on a family vacation to the Badlands when I was fourteen, only on that trip we stopped and spent a night in Mitchell, home of the Corn Palace. Today we hit Mitchell and keep on rolling. All afternoon and into the evening the scenery is the same: the highway's broken white center line, semitrailers streaming west in plumes of exhaust, the flatness of the plains. Checking our mileage, I'm amazed by how far we've come and how far we still have to go. Riddle, Oregon, where my father and I will meet the homestead's owners at a gas station and follow them into the homestead, is 2,316 miles from my little hometown in Indiana. I can no more fathom this distance than I can fathom the distance from Earth to the moon. And though I have poured over the manual Bradley sent me and spent the last few months reading everything I can get my hands on about the Pacific Northwest, I still don't totally know what to expect. The moon might actually be more familiar a place to me than the Rogue River canyon.

What is my father thinking as we drive along? I haven't the foggiest idea. Perhaps he's nervous about what could happen to me living alone for seven months in the woods. Somehow I doubt it. He stares out the window, taking in the changing scenery. He's thinking about whether a steelhead will take a night crawler. He's thinking this experience will make a man out of me. He's thinking that after the thirty-two years he spent in the pharmaceutical industry, there's no better way to enjoy retirement than by getting out and seeing a piece of the country. Or maybe he's not thinking anything, just resting and staring out the window at the changing scenery.

It's a comfort having him along. From time to time, I just look at him—this man I've always known. His shiny bald head. Sideburns beginning to turn silver. Big Popeye forearms with their gold hairs. This is the man who bathed my brother and me when we were small enough to fit in the tub together.

I've invited him along because I need help with the drive. I also want him to feel proud of me and to see this as an accomplishment. He's along, however, to make sure I'm not getting in over my head.

Fathers and sons.

On the second morning of the trip, we wake road weary and dazed in a Motel 6 in Rapid City, South Dakota. The day dawns bright and clear, a lucky break in April, and scenery that yesterday ran on an endless loop has somehow shifted overnight. We're in the Black Hills region. Along the horizon are pine-studded ridges and steep granite outcroppings. Touristy billboards tout Black Hills gold and jackalopes. Soon we cross into Wyoming, clipping the northeast corner: Gillette, Sheridan, the Bighorn Mountains. The land flattens again, but it's not like the fertile pastures of Iowa or Illinois. It's dry and dusty, wind beaten, dotted with scrub. I watch the long wire fences roll by and count pronghorn among the black cattle.

Midmorning we cross into eastern Montana, and my father perks up. We have entered the Crow Indian Reservation.

"I mean, we won the war," he says, waving a hand over the steering wheel at the surrounding hills and forest, the scattering of outbuildings far from the road. "I don't see why we don't just take all this back. We ought to be using this land for something."

"Just take it back?"

"*Something.*"

In Billings we stop for lunch at a Pizza Hut, gas up, and switch drivers. Not long after that, we come to a spectacle that makes it clear we're now in the West: the snow-covered Crazy Mountains in full sun.

From the Crazies it's not much farther (a couple hours) to Three Forks, Montana, where my father's friend the Six Million Dollar Man—a moniker earned after some oil deal he made in Wyoming—has offered to put us up for the night. His plush three-story house sits on 340 acres of sprawling marsh between two forks of the Jefferson River. In the distance the snow-covered peaks of three separate mountain ranges appear in faint relief: the Gallatins, the Bridgers, and Big Sky. It's a beautiful day for April, sixty and sunny, and up at the house, the Six Million Dollar Man greets my father and me with firm handshakes. He's wearing a flannel shirt, jeans, work boots. An unlit cigarillo hangs from his lip. We stand around the little trout pond he's had dug in his front yard, watching fish rise to the surface, and when he asks about the origins of our trip I tell him the story: I've somehow won a writing contest, and the prize is seven months as caretaker of a backcountry homestead in Oregon. When he asks what kind of writing I do, I say fiction. He's just finished reading *Close Range* by E. Annie Proulx.

"Those are some tough stories," I say.

"That's Wyoming," he says.

"Who owns all them mountains?" my father wonders aloud, gesturing toward a distant range of snowy peaks.

The Six Million Dollar Man shrugs, says he doesn't know, says the government probably holds the lease. I tell him how impressed I'd been by the Crazy Mountains after the flatness of Billings. "The Crazies," the Six Million Dollar Man says, raising his eyebrows, nodding. "The Crazies are beautiful."

That night, after a meal at a rib joint in the little town of Willow Springs, I bed down in a sleeping bag in the Six Million Dollar Man's sunroom and can see huge wintergreen stars twinkling in the sky. Strangely, I don't feel far from home at all tonight. If anything, I feel closer. I think of the miles my father and I have driven, that life and land and sky, those millions of stories colliding like atoms in places I'll never know. By comparison, my own life seems small. My worries and fears, my hopes and dreams and aspirations. One more speck of dust in an infinite universe.

The next morning my father and I wake to snow. The flakes are dime sized and falling furiously. Nothing to do but take off and hope for the best (and pull over if we have to pull over), we pile into my truck and wave good-bye to the Six Million Dollar Man and his river-island homestead. Despite the snow, we make halfway decent time, flying down i-90 in a convoy of eighteen-wheelers. Signs appear for Butte and Deer Lodge. The road rises, drops, dips, and curves. Throngs of dark, snow-covered pines lean into the wind. Craggy peaks and ridges crowd the sky. The scenery so challenges my midwestern sense of scale and proportion that as morning gives way to afternoon I have no real appreciation of how much time is passing. As we round one bend, the city of Missoula appears, its grid of streets and houses nestled snugly in the valley below. Then we shoot north to the tip of Idaho and Lake Coeur d'Alene. We zip through the heart of Spokane and afterward are surrounded by wheat fields that stretch to the horizon.

All afternoon, I keep a foot on the gas. We cross the Columbia River at Umatilla and head west on I-84, cleaving to a series of high bluffs that look out over the water. Another few hours snowcapped Mount Hood appears, followed by the Portland skyline and a snarl of commuter traffic. Everything here is lush and green—lawns, hillsides, trees. South of the city, we pass acre after acre of blooming tulips, like a postcard from Holland. The sky is blue, the clouds full and gray. Then it's down to the town of Corvallis and out to the coast. We drive by bucolic pastures and hobby farms, where gorgeous black and white horses stand perfectly still in fields of tall grass, where black cattle kneel under the spreading arms of an oak.

Since leaving the Six Million Dollar Man's house, my father and I have been watching the sky, calculating mileage and wondering if we'd arrive at our destination tonight in time to watch the sunset over the Pacific.

"Well, what do you think?" I say.

"Maybe," my father says.

Our final stretch of highway winds its way through the fir-shrouded coast range with the light fast fading.

About the time I think there's no way we'll make it before dark, the highway spits us out of the mountains and stuns us with a view of the ocean from a lookout on Highway 101 at Waldport. The water churns like a sloshing cauldron, and the air all around us is gray. But there, far out on the horizon, glows a slender band of pinkish orange where the sun has just now dipped below the edge of the world.

IN TYPICAL MIDWESTERN FASHION, my father and I have arrived a day early and now must decide what to do with the extra time.

There are any number of options along the coast: hike up Cape Perpetua, near Yachats, to the big lookout over the water; check out Sea Lion Caves farther south; drive dune buggies down at the Oregon Dunes National Recreational Area. In our hotel lobby we look at pamphlets and decide to drive another three or four hours south on Highway 101 to see redwood trees. We've driven this far, what's another few hours?

Highway 101 winds its way along the coast, offering stunning views of the water and the beach. Towns come and go: Coos Bay, Port Orford, Pistol River. I see old men in rain slickers mending fishing nets out on long, rickety piers. The weather is overcast and cool. The ocean is the color of pencil lead.

At the California border there's a checkpoint, and we think it might be a drunk-driving initiative of some kind, or possibly a manhunt. When we pull up to the officer in charge, he asks if we've brought any produce with us across the border. The confusion must show on my face. "Produce," he says. "Fruits and veggies." Then he explains that it's an effort to keep invasive insect species out of the state's billion-dollar orchards. We have some apples, I tell him.

"From the grocery?"

"Yeah," I say.

He waves us through.

After the checkpoint, we zip down to the Jedediah Smith Redwoods State Park and take a driving tour. It dawns on us, as midwestern tourists, that we don't really know what a redwood looks like. Sure, we've seen the iconic pictures—cars driving through the enormous trunks—but nothing around here looks like that. The trees are extremely large with a red tint to their bark, but are they redwoods? We just don't know. And it's sad that we don't know. We pull into an empty campground parking lot and decide to walk around a while, stretch our legs. Whether the trees all around us are redwoods or not, this is an eerily beautiful place: wisps of fog flutter in the canopy of trees; a damp pine-needle smell rises from our footsteps. We have walked maybe fifty feet when we come to a picnic table whose legs have rotted out from under it. On the table's surface is the unmistakable evidence of bears: a series of long claw marks in the soft wood. And on a nearby tree trunk at eye level is a sign with a picture of a bear: YOU ARE IN BEAR COUNTRY. BE BEAR AWARE. I am suddenly unaccountably afraid.

In my heart of hearts, I know it's ridiculous. I should be able to point to a tree and identify it as a redwood. I should be able to take a stroll in bear country without a bad feeling in the pit of my stomach. But right now—just a day before meeting the owners of the homestead and getting set up to live in bear country for seven months—I just can't. I'm afraid. There is an actual lump in my throat.

We take a last look at the picnic table with the claw marks and casually decide to cut our stroll short, keep driving.

As we head up Highway 199, back to Grants Pass (where we'll stay the night before meeting the owners in Riddle the next day and following them into the homestead), my cowardice sickens me. We've come all this way. Across the Great Plains, through the Rockies, along the Columbia River Gorge. Come all this way and for what? To be scared out of a campground by claw marks that for all we know could be ten years old? How in the world am I supposed to be a caretaker of a backcountry homestead when I can't even stand in bear country for five minutes without getting a lump in my throat? It doesn't bode well, and the whole way north I'm on edge, cranky. We take a room at a Motel 6, and because it's still early, my father wants to go out, explore the city of Grants Pass. Maybe get some more groceries for the week we'll spend at the homestead together. Maybe find the post office. A Laundromat. I'm not having any part of it.

"Go out if you want," I tell him.

"You don't want to look around?"

"No."

What I want to do is lay on the flimsy bed with the curtains drawn tight and sulk. Finally, my father shrugs and says he thinks he saw a donut shop down the street; he's going to check it out. He'll be back.

Then the room is mine, and as has happened to me so often in cheap hotels, in towns far from home, a great loneliness descends. I listen to the traffic on Sixth Street, its steady grind, and every once in a while someone walks past my door. I hear the gentle sound of footsteps, murmuring voices. It reminds me of nights as a kid when I'd lie awake in bed listening to the sounds of my mother and father settling in for the evening, feeling as though everything were right in the world and mourning its goodness, never wanting anything to change. And also nights in my early twenties, alone in an efficiency apartment after a divorce, hounded by doubt and regret. From the window of that place, I could see the underside of a bridge that spanned the Wabash River. A homeless man lived there, and one day, walking by on my way to teach a class at Purdue, I saw three big square-cut swatches of sod the man had stolen from a yard somewhere. He'd been sleeping on them. There was an indentation where he'd lain his head.

I think about that homeless man, about my divorce, about that era in my life when things had felt so shaky and adrift: that was four years ago. Now I'm starting a new era. When I first decided to enter this contest some part of me knew that I'd win. Not because I'm the world's greatest writer, but because I needed it. That was the story I'd been telling. That more than anyone else, I needed it.

I try to remind myself of that.

It doesn't help.

Lying on the bed, thumbing through Bradley's manual, I go over the rules and regulations, the warnings about wildfires and disease-carrying ticks, what to do in the event of serious injury, the explanation of the water system, the hand-drawn maps into the homestead, the two hundred hours of chores I'm to fulfill in order to complete my hour-a-day caretaking duties. Should anything go wrong—should a pipe burst or a bear break into the cabin—it's up to me to deal with it. What happens if I can't? What happens if I come up short on character? What if I fail everyone?

It's maybe an hour before my father returns from his walk to the donut shop. We're both ready for dinner and head across the street to a restaurant. It's dusk. The sun has dropped below the cloud ceiling and is shining wanly on the low, folded mountains surrounding town. There is a freshness in the air, a coolness. Over a dinner of hamburgers and french fries and Cokes, my father informs me that he met a local at the donut shop who said you couldn't find better halfpounder steelhead fishing than on the Rogue River. Who said once upon a time it was a big gold-mining river. "I may have to do a little panning for gold," my father says, between bites of hamburger. And I tell him: he'll get his chance, that tomorrow's the big day. "I'd like to find me a big gold nugget," he says. "Wouldn't that be something? A gold nugget?" I tell him: it would.

It's spitting rain when my father and I pull into the gas station near Riddle, Oregon. Big wisps of steam rise from the surrounding mountains. The Douglas firs are wet and green. This is what Bradley calls "Last Gas" in the manual—from here on in, some forty-five miles of bumpy logging roads, it's Bureau of Land Management (BLM) numbered roads and bridges over little creeks: Middle Creek, Cow Creek, Riffle Creek.

We're early again. We fill up with gas and back into a parking spot in a corner of the lot. We watch logging trucks roll by on the highway. They are loaded down with long, skinny trunks, oversized Lincoln Logs.

With the engine switched off, the truck is chilly. I'm wearing blue jeans with big holes in the knees, a thick flannel shirt, a barn coat, steel-toed boots. There is no backcountry in Indiana, and this is my best guess as to what one might wear if there were. It's my poor imitation of the farmers I grew up around, out combining corn in the late-October chill. I suppose I could have done some research on the Web or bought a copy of *Outdoor Magazine* or *Backpacker*, but somewhere down deep I already knew that nothing betrayed one's inexperience in the woods quite like getting decked out in the latest expensive and unnecessary wilderness accoutrements. Not to mention that I didn't have the money. I'd been house sitting half the year for a retired poetry professor, teaching a few sections of English 101 at Purdue as an adjunct, saving every last penny—I couldn't see spending a hundred bucks on hiking boots.

Likewise with my truck. Bradley had suggested a four-wheel drive, a little Toyota or maybe a Jeep, but in a homemade video he and Frank sent, I thought I heard Frank say that his rig was two-wheel drive and he'd never had a problem getting in and out of the homestead. So when I had to acquire a truck, I bought a fairly new two-wheel drive GMC from a mattress salesman who used it to make his deliveries. A standard midwestern rig, big and square and durable, it was the kind of truck you could imagine parked six deep at any small-town café in rural Indiana on a Friday night. I even liked the color: slate gray. Nothing flashy or glitzy, just a vehicle to take you where you wanted to go. Why pay more for a truck with more miles and more wear simply because it had four-wheel drive? It wasn't like I'd be off-roading. When I'd made my mandatory visit to the homestead last summer, I rented an SUV, and it felt like overkill. The roads were bumpy and I had to watch out for fallen rocks that could puncture a tire, but they were roads like any I'd ever driven before.

From "Last Gas" Bradley's manual says it's another two hours of logging roads into the homestead. My father and I sit in the truck, wait. When the windows steam, I roll them down and breathe in the pulpy, sulfuric smell of a pulp mill. It's not so terribly different from the corn-processing plant back home, the stink of sweet gold kernels being melted for syrup. It's strangely comforting.

"Is that them?" my father says after a time, pointing to a rusty Toyota pulling in, three middle-aged men up front.

The truck pulls up to a pump, and the three of them hop out. I recognize Bradley and Joe Green, last year's resident caretaker, from my mandatory trip to the homestead. In his wire-frame glasses and John Berryman beard Joe Green had peppered me with questions I didn't understand about soldering copper pipe. Bradley—tan, bald, clean shaven—laughingly opened a sliding glass door on the deck of the upper house to show me where a bear had tried to paw its way in. "See that scratch?" he said, pointing to a long arcing scar in the glass. "Now what's the only thing sharp enough to scratch glass? That's right. Diamonds! We got us a diamond-clawed bear!"

The other man with Bradley and Joe Green is Bradley's brother, Frank. As I understand it, Frank is a well-known ceramist who runs an artist program up the coast, the Sitka Center for Art and Ecology. He is tall and lanky, wearing blue jeans and boots, a sock cap bunched on the back of his head.

My father asks again if that's them, then looks at me, waiting. Up until now, I could have called it off. Chickened out. But against what feels like my better judgment, I tell him that's them and get out and wave hello to everyone. Frank introduces himself with a handshake. Bradley pounds me on the back. Joe nods. I introduce them to my father and hear myself saying I'm glad to see them all.

"That your rig?" Bradley says, eyeballing my truck. A look of deep concentration—perhaps irritation—has spread across his face. "You'll ruin my road with that monster."

He pulls off his wool beret and runs a hand over his bald head, pinches his lips with his forefinger and thumb, keeps staring at my truck. Frank, the taller of the two, pulls off his sock cap, folds it in his hands, says the roads get awfully, awfully muddy in the spring and worries that I might get stuck. Joe Green, in a rain slicker, a crumpled fedora, points at the tires. "Street treads," he says.

Bradley's chewing his bottom lip, thinking it over. In his gray work pants and boots, his scuffed jacket, his wool beret, he looks like any other Oregonian I've encountered in the last day and a half. There's something in his countenance, though—his arch seriousness, the scrutiny with which he's considering the details of our trip into the homestead—that makes me think of a general on the eve of battle. As a greenhorn from Indiana who knows next to nothing about the world he's entering, I'm intimidated as hell but at the same time deeply grateful. He tells me I'm going to need mud and snow tires. Then he asks me if I have chains. He says that I'm going to need chains.

"You should've called me," he says. "I could've told you—you need four-wheel drive. It's muddy as hell in the spring."

"I'll get new tires."

"Then again," he says, lifting his eyebrows and shrugging, "as dry as it's been, you may not have a problem. They might even close your road for fire precaution. Then you'll have to get a permit from the BLM. They might even close off the river to rafters. That's how bad it is. Middle of a ten-year drought."

I nod as though I understand.

Bradley sighs.

For now at least, we're just going to have to make due. Last report from John Daniel, who spent the winter in solitude at the homestead, was that the road was dry and clear. We'll have to take him at his word. We'll go slow. If I get stuck or start to slip and slide, Frank's got a big steel chain, and we can connect our rigs. It's something they have apparently had to do before. Bradley and Frank share a glance and a laugh. There's a story I don't quite catch about a writer whose rig wouldn't stop sliding on the downhill slope. They tethered their rigs with the chain—the writer's vehicle out in front and Bradley back behind, with his rig in 4WD low range, and riding the brakes. Or else it was the other way around, and the writer kept braking every time Bradley stepped on the gas. I don't totally catch it because the two of them are laughing so hard, remembering, and because I'm glad they're laughing, and because I'm relieved to hear I'm not the first greenhorn writer they've had to deal with. For a while there, the way Bradley scowled at my truck, I thought we might have to delay the trip. I thought: here we are, day one, and you've already screwed up.

2

THE BIG QUIET

ON THE TWO-HOUR SLOG INTO THE homestead, I stick close to Frank's little red Toyota and take only the quickest side glances. On the horizon it's mountain after mountain, low and craggy, primordial looking. At road's edge, it's a five-hundred-foot drop straight down. My father and I have gotten quiet again. Only this isn't the Zen-like oneness with the road we'd experienced at 75 mph on the interstate. This is the quiet of reverence and awe. The remoteness of where we're going has become real.

An hour into the drive, the rain turns to snow. Big wet flakes hit my windshield and melt, are brushed aside by the wipers. My father pulls out his camera, takes a picture. The way the snow looks, how slowly it falls against this backdrop of Douglas firs and mountains, is something to remember.

I take a mental picture: the way the snow sticks to the treads in Frank's snow tires and then falls out of them.

I should have realized before this moment that my GMC is rear-wheel drive. On steep, slick, muddy roads—with no weight in the back—how am I supposed to get any traction? And why wasn't this something I thought of before? Especially since it was right there, in black-and-white, in the manual Bradley sent me. When I am here alone I will have to pay more attention to these kinds of details. There won't be anybody to pull my truck out of a ditch if I slide off the road, and there won't be any phone to call for help. The thought is daunting. I've never spent more than a day or two in solitude. I've never changed a tire. But I tell myself that I'm a writer, and any writer worth his weight in salt must seek out these kinds of encounters with solitude and self. Like John Muir going it alone in the Sierra Nevada. Thoreau at Walden. The kinds of delusions of grandeur that help me step forward into my fear.

It's past three o'clock when we finally arrive at the turnoff for the homestead. The forest is dark and drippy, smelling of wet fir needles and the hot brake pads of my truck. At the first of two gates we stop, and I roll down my window, breathe it all in. Around us are Douglas firs with wet black trunks, giant arcing ferns, mossy rocks. The quiet is enormous, penetrating.

From where the BLM road meets the homestead's driveway it's a winding two-mile descent to the houses. We pass through one gate, then another. At a clearing where some trees had fallen last autumn we stop and look out at a pair of black-tailed deer grazing in a wet mountain meadow. Farther down the driveway we come to a little pond that provides water for the garden and fire suppression. Bradley points out a cistern back among the ferns, says this is where my drinking water comes from, right out of the mountains. Around the corner from the pond is the upper house, where Frank and Bradley stay during their infrequent visits. I'd seen my first black bear here with Bradley when I visited last summer. Beautifully sleek, it emerged from the forest and nosed through the long grass in the orchard below the deck.

The lower house, the caretaker's house—where I'll be staying—is a quarter-mile farther down the drive. Built into the hillside on wooden stilts, it's a good-size modern structure with a skinny metal chimney and a solar panel for heating hot water. In the side yard a blue propane pig squats in the shade of a Douglas fir, and—twenty yards below—a pair of gnarled apple trees frame the entrance to the garden, where John Daniel's winter vegetable crop is going gangbusters. Big purple heads of cabbage, bushy mustard plants, rows of collard greens.

The house is complete with a solitary writer's every need and convenience: a kitchen stocked with dishes, pots and pans, utensils; a propane-powered oven range and fridge; indoor plumbing—shower, sink, septic tank for the toilet; skylight in the bedroom; and a deck overlooking the river canyon.

As the five of us get busy unloading boxes from my truck—my clothes and books and supplies—I keep looking around at everything, unable to quite believe I'll be living here. Bradley's perfunctory safety overview only intensifies the feeling. Here are the copper pipes that run from the stove to the hot water tank (don't ever have a fire if those pipes are empty, he says, because they will melt); here's how the propane wall lamps light (check them from time to time for gas leaks); here are the homestead's guns and ammo (a .22 Joe Green used to plunk the digger squirrels hell-bent on eating his beans, and a big 30.06 for dealing with Mr. Bear). It is all too much to remember at once, and when I say as much to Bradley, he says that that's why he types up his manual. Everything I need to know is in there.

In the few minutes of daylight we have left, we decide we'd better see how my truck will handle climbing up this muddy driveway. There's a turnaround below the lower house Bradley wants me to use. I've driven in plenty of inclement weather in Indiana—snowstorms, pounding rain—and don't quite understand why they are making such a big deal of a little mud. So I get behind the wheel, fire the engine, and drive down to the turnaround. On my way back, the first few seconds, everything's fine. Then my back end starts to slide. I give it gas. My RPMS flare.

"Forget it!" Bradley calls. "Just forget it!"

I get out and survey the damage. My street treads have torn up a healthy swatch of Bradley's road, and I'm stuck.

"Tell you what I'd do," Bradley says, nodding, serious. "When you get back to Grants Pass next week, find yourself a dealership and see if you can't make a trade. You need four-wheel drive in all this mud."

For a temporary fix, we take a few slabs of busted-up concrete lying by the side of the house and pile them in my truck bed. About five hundred pounds worth. Then Frank gets the chain out of his truck, backs down and tethers us together. He tows me to the upper house, where there's crushed rock in the driveway. It's decided that on Sunday, when they're leaving, I'll follow them out and park at the top of the road. From the top of the road, my father and I shouldn't have any trouble.

At the upper house, with my truck pulled off to the side and out of the way, I thank Frank, Bradley, and Joe Green for their help. They'll be by in the morning, Bradley says, bright and early. We've got a big day ahead of us—hopefully the rain holds off. My father and I wave and start back down the driveway home. I don't really want to trade in my truck, but if Bradley thinks that's what I should do, then that's probably what I should do. In the meantime, it has gotten much cooler in the couple hours we've been here. I wonder if it might snow. Back at the house, my father and I peel off our muddy boots and start a fire in the woodstove. For dinner it's Dinty Moore Beef Stew. I light one of the propane wall lamps, and we sit at a small chipped table, watching the sky darken over the river canyon. I still can't get over the quiet. It's out there, like some enormous animal, and all that keeps me from joining it—from being consumed by it—is the soft sputtering of the propane wall lamps and the sound of my father slurping his dinner.

I SLEEP ON THE FLOOR by the stove and wake at first light, chilly, stiff, anxious to start the day. In the back bedroom my father is snoring. Careful not to wake him, I get up and slip out onto the deck. There's a low mist on the mountains, and it's hazy, cool, quiet. A light dusting of snow whitens one of the high ridges.

I listen for Bradley and the others at the upper house. Either they're not up and moving, or I just can't hear them.

I take these few moments to dash off a quick letter to some friends back home in Indiana. It's only by trying to describe what I see that I really start to see. The light radiating off a flowering pear tree in the garden. The hand-hewn cedar shakes on the homestead's hundred-year-old barn. As I write my letter, three Columbia black-tailed deer—yearling bucks that I mistakenly identify as female because they have not yet sprouted their antlers—emerge from the forest and start nibbling grass between the skid marks my truck left in the driveway. They are cautious but calm, at home here, looking up every few seconds, then taking another mouthful of fresh spring grass. I watch them blink and chew. They sniff the air. Their ears twitch. As they drift down the lane and duck one by one under a rotting split-rail fence en route to a nearby salt block, puffs of breath steam out of their nostrils.

For breakfast my father and I cook a pot of oatmeal. Afterward, we clean out our bowls, rinse them off, and set them in a strainer. When I came to visit last summer, an art student of Frank's (having come to the homestead to help Bradley with some chores) had just had the back window of his car busted out by a bear. What was in there that the bear wanted so badly? A candy-bar wrapper. By comparison, a bowl of oatmeal is a feast. We don't know if the bears are out of hibernation, but there is a good probability that they are or will be soon. We don't want to take any chances.

"You see this article?" my father says.

He's standing in front of a plywood wall onto which someone has tacked a few poems and news articles. My father, a white dishtowel slung over his shoulder, reads the article over the top of his bifocals.

It's about a man whose car plummeted off a nearby road and into a giant snowbank, trapping him. He managed to live for several days. On every scrap of paper he could find—receipt stubs, envelopes—he furiously scribbled a good-bye to his family. It's a cautionary tale about this place, these backcountry roads, but it's also a story about writing with a sense of urgency and purpose.

After the breakfast dishes and the news article, my father plunks down in the La-Z-Boy recliner facing the mountains and closes his eyes, relaxes. I go out onto the deck again. The sun is all the way up now, shooting a low, slanting ray across the garden and the barn and the split-rail corral fence. I can hear people moving around at the upper house, Bradley shouting jovially. In a little while, Frank's Toyota comes putt-putting down the road, Frank and Bradley inside, Joe Green riding on the tailgate. I'm ready to do whatever it is they need me to do. That's the frame of mind I'm in today. It doesn't matter if I'm tired or cold or wet, I'm going to gut it out.

One of the day's first orders of business is chainsaw training, and Frank wastes no time on the lesson. He produces a chainsaw from the back of his truck, marches down the lane to a young madrone, slips on a pair of safety goggles, and fells the tree. "I tell you, I never liked the looks of that one," he says.

"No?"

The Big Quiet

"Got on my nerves."

I'm made to put on special neon-orange chainsaw leg chaps ("Just wear the pants," Bradley admonishes when I balk) that are like bullet-proof vests for your legs. I make a few cuts down the tree trunk.

And so goes the morning. Down in the barn, I'm shown the garden implements—the rototiller, hoses, nippers—and given lessons on aerating the soil between rows of grapevines in the garden. I'm shown the homestead's lawnmower. Bradley tells me I'll need to mow the roadside and around the houses (a good fifty feet) three times: by the first of May, June, and July. In the garden we stop a moment to look at the new and improved fence Bradley and Joe Green erected last summer—an eight-foot monolith of barbed wire and steel, constructed after a bear broke in and nearly destroyed a sour-pie cherry tree. Later this spring, Bradley says, he's going to string a solar-electric wire around the fence and hang a bunch of bear licks.

"What's a bear lick?" I ask.

"A bear lick?"

"Yeah."

"A little sheet of tin you sort of hang off the wire." He twitches his eyebrows and grins. "You put some peanut butter on there, man. And when Mr. Bear takes a lick—zap!—right in the tongue!"

How would a tongue-stung bear react? The five of us stand around the garden and theorize. It might just turn tail and run. Or maybe it would get pissed and thrash the fence. Personally, I don't think that a onetime jolt of electricity to the tongue is enough to flip off a bear's curiosity switch. But I suppose that's not really the point—whether the licks actually work. If anything, they're an expression of Bradley's love and admiration for the bears. He wants to see how they'll outsmart him.

After the bear licks, everything blurs. It's up to the pond for a lesson on the water system: how to clean the springhouse and change out the brass screen; how to replace and repair PVC pipe; how to spray the pond with Cutrine, if it needs it, for relief of green slime. Bradley points across the pond at a meadow filled with ferns and Douglas fir saplings. He'd like me to pull the saplings, a reclamation project of sorts, and mow the ferns. Then sometime this spring I should walk the road and remove debris from the five culverts below the upper gate. I should cut back any encroaching trees and blackberry canes. There will be leaves to rake—madrone leaves in August and oak leaves in October. Gutters will need scraping out. Fir needles will need to be swept off the decks of both the upper and lower houses. And the list goes on. Not an excessive amount of work by any stretch—really, it's just an hour a day of routine caretaking—but I would be lying if I said I weren't also slightly overwhelmed. Growing up back home in Indiana, I'd always had to mow grass and help gather and haul in firewood. I spent my summers as a teenager, from thirteen to eighteen, working on corn-detasseling crews. Hard work isn't some strange new thing to me. I've just never before done it primarily for, or by, myself.

AFTER THE MORNING'S ORIENTATION, we take an hour for lunch and then head down to the river. This is what I've been waiting for. Below the lower house, below the splintery corral fence and its meadow of chest-high grass, a foot trail eases into the forest and disappears. We walk single file, Frank, Bradley, and Joe in the lead, my father and I in the rear. We carry fishing rods, small packs with water, extra flies. It's raining. Not the hard spring rain of an Indiana thunderstorm, but the gentle, relentless misting of the Pacific Northwest. The rain makes everything shine—ferns uncurling along the trail, moss on the trees. Every so often Frank or Bradley stops to point something out to me: marks on a fallen tree where a bear has scratched it open for grubs, an herb you can make a tea from called yerba buena, a wildflower called a shooting star, whose soft purple petals flare out in a pattern that brings to mind its namesake in the night sky.

Halfway to the river, the trail opens up to a wide meadow. I'd hiked this way with John Daniel last summer, and the grass was brown, dry, dead. Today it's wet and green. Up ahead, Bradley points to something. I look and see two dozen black-tailed deer drifting across the meadow, some of them bending their heads to eat, some sniffing the air, some lazily meandering along their scent trails in the grass. They move as though of one body, like clouds, breaking apart, coming back together.

On the other side of the meadow, the trail through the forest—the simple dirt path we've been following—peters out. We fan apart and pick our individual ways through the trees, heading down, down, down. I become aware of a soft, far-off roar: the Rogue River.

We see it first from several hundred feet above. The water is greenish black, glassy, with foam frothing in the rapids, swirling around big eddies and draws, plunging westward. I have no idea how to fish such a huge river, and when we see it up close I am even more bewildered. The Rogue thrashes and bucks, surges, swells, roars, rolling the great boulders on its bottom, wearing down the metamorphic rock of its shores. The sound of water on rock. Lapping, dripping, draining. Sloshing. Gurgling. If you slipped and fell into the river, its current would carry you off like a twig, snap you in two.

There's nothing too complicated about fly fishing, Bradley tells me. It's a matter of physics—the weight of the line, the surface tension of the water, the angle of your rod. We march out to a flat, rocky bar, and he ties a fly to my outfit, shows me how it's done. With a few easy sweeps of the arm, my neon-orange line slashes the air like some kind of graceful, snapping whip. I watch as the fly, just a pinch of feathers, thread, and glue, flits out over the water and lands with the tiniest splash. Bradley tugs it in with his left hand, his right hand holding the rod over the river at a forty-five-degree angle. He's facing downstream, and that's important. Dead things float on the surface, sucked along by the current. Living things swim against it. The fly comes back to him, and he raises his arm, yanks the line back behind his head, and sends it out again. His fly swims through the greenish black water in short bursts, like a minnow, and suddenly there's a flash of silver, the fly disappears, and Bradley's rod doubles over. He's got one, a beautiful fourteen-inch steelhead. He lands it at the water's edge, wetting his hands before touching the fish. The hook is fastened tightly in a corner of its mouth. He takes out the hook, holds the fish up to me.

"Now," Bradley says, releasing the fish and shaking his hands dry. "Think you can do that?"

I tell him I'll try, and he hands me my rod. That's the extent of lesson number one. The rest of the afternoon, as the sunlight advances and retreats through a seemingly endless armada of rain clouds, I stand on the bar and try to imitate Bradley's cast. I meet with modest success: I don't hook myself.

Otherwise, I have a hard time. My line tangles into a bird's nest around my reel. I snag the riverside willows behind me and lose my fly, have to tie on another. Though I alter the angle of my rod and play with the firmness and snap of my wrist, I can't seem to get any distance on my cast. The one time I manage a halfway decent attempt, I turn a fish—but I've done such a poor job of tying my hook, it snaps right off in the fish's mouth and leaves me holding an empty line. Thankfully, I've got time. That's what's keeping me sane today. The spring run should last another couple of weeks, and I'll be here for two months of the autumn run. There's time to learn.

In the meantime, the fish are beautiful. The tiny orange lichens on the rocks are beautiful. The rocks themselves, their jagged angles, their sparkling variegated guts—I could spend all day just looking at them.

And maybe that's the point of a place like this—the chance to follow your desire, to spend a day looking at rocks.

To be childlike.

Which is something else, whether he knows it or not, that Bradley is teaching me this weekend. Later in the day, we're standing on a gravel bar when twenty yards to our east, in among some boulders, a great blue heron lands in a runoff pool. We watch him prowl the shallows a moment, peering intently into the murky water. His feathers are slate gray, exquisite. He cautiously dips his bill.

Bradley says to go get a better look.

"Sneak up on him," he says.

There was a great blue heron who lived at our little farm pond back home in Indiana, and we almost never saw it up close—at the first sign of a human it always bolted.

"He'll fly off," I say.

"Just try it."

So at Bradley's insistence, I pick my way over the rocks, keeping close to the river's edge and out of the bird's line of sight, until finally I'm on one side of a big boulder and the bird is on the other, ten feet away. Quiet as I can, I peek over the top of the rock. The heron is magnificent: its S-shaped neck and long yellow bill; its soft blue-gray feathers; the reddish brown of its underside. It looks back at me with a large metallic-yellow eye, one leg slightly bent. Surprised, scowling, the look on the bird's face says: what in the hell are *you* doing here? Before I can offer an explanation, the heron spreads its ample, awkward wings and lumbers into the sky.

When it's finally time for us to head home up the mountain, I take a last long look at the river. I want to remember every ripple and rock, every grain of sand. We've all caught fish today, even my father and me. He found a night crawler, parked himself before a big frothing eddy, and hooked the biggest steelhead of the day. I had help from Frank, who took my arm in his and sent my fly to the river's far side where it was promptly snapped up. A wonderful day all around. Even as we switchback up the trail, climbing some eight hundred vertical feet in three-quarters of a mile—sweating through our shirts, breathing hard, hearts thumping—there is no denying the day's goodness, the goodness of this place. Up the mountain we go, the five of us, late of a spring afternoon, one foot in front of the other, sweaty and exhausted, achy, happy, glad. Emerging finally from the dark of the forest trail into the gray half-light of dusk, the homestead's meadow of tall yellow grasses is a welcome sight. The flowering fruit trees in the garden. The cedar shakes on the hundred-year-old barn. Before leaving this afternoon, my father banked a fire in the stove, and this is perhaps the most welcome sight of all: the lower house snug against the mountainside, a line of blue smoke dribbling from the chimney.

3

BREAKING INTO
THE BACKCOUNTRY

ON SUNDAY MORNING WHEN IT'S TIME to drive to the top of the road to say good-bye to Frank and Bradley and Joe Green, I do so with reluctance. For one, none of us is sure whether the five hundred pounds of busted-up concrete we loaded into the back of my pickup will be enough to keep me from getting stuck. Further, I have to ask: don't these guys realize I'm not prepared, competent, or ready? One way or another in the last two days they've each communicated to me something I haven't yet accepted, namely, that the homestead itself will teach me what I need to know in order to go it alone. I want to believe them. I do. And I know down deep that the only thing worse than failing as the homestead's caretaker would be to quit before getting started. But, by God, there is a very real part of me that would like nothing better than to thank them, apologize, and turn tail for home.

It takes us a good ten to fifteen minutes to climb the two miles up and out of the homestead, and despite some slipping and sliding, we make it without any real problems. Just below the upper gate, I park in a grove of Douglas firs and get out, look around. Forest, sky, a rutted one-lane logging road. I ask if my truck will be safe here for the week, so far from the cabins. Bradley thinks it will. Frank, too. Joe Green says his wife parked her car in this same spot last summer, fearing the driveway too bumpy for her suspension. When she returned the car was just fine—ringed by a handful of spent shotgun shells but just fine.

After a few minutes of looking around, telling stories, laughing—all of them reluctant to leave—Frank says they'd better pack it in and encourages me to write something beautiful; and Bradley tells me that the place is mine now, that I'm its owner and should act as such; and Joe Green, stroking his beard and looking at me over the top of his wire-frame eyeglasses, says that he envies me. Then, nothing else left to say, they pile into Frank's pickup, wave good-bye, and disappear around the bend.

"Those guys are something," my father says as we turn and start back on foot. "You fit in pretty good."

"Think so?"

"Yeah. You're all crazy."

I ask him what he thinks about Bradley's idea—that once we get back to town we trade in my truck for something more appropriate to these roads. He says we didn't have much trouble today. The concrete helped. And with that we somehow decide the truck I've bought will be fine. If the rains come back in force after I've dropped my father off next week and the roads turn to soup, I'll just have to wait out the weather.

The rest of the walk home we talk about other things: fishing, our chances of seeing a bear. My father says he still wants to pan for gold, says that he could see flakes of it foaming up on the sand, and would like to take some home. It feels good to talk casually, to forget for a while the solitude that lurks ahead of me. And I can understand why Frank, Bradley, and Joe had all been so reluctant to leave, to go back home to their lives. It's shaping up to be another gorgeous cool spring day along the Rogue, and the river is full of fish.

Upon returning to the cabin, my father and I use the satellite phone to call my mother back in Indiana and let her know we've made it to the homestead, that everything's okay. She's been taking care of my dying grandmother the past two years. It's the last grueling stages of liver cancer, and in recent weeks hospice has been called in. My father and I knew when we left for this trip that she didn't have much longer to live. "It's over," my mother says, the phone line crackling with static. "She died this morning." And my father and I both realize—because we talked about this possibility before leaving—that we will miss the funeral. The irony hits hard. I've come here to be alone, but right now it's my mother who's alone.

After the phone call I realize that not being with the rest of my family at my grandmother's funeral—to grieve with them, to tell stories, to laugh and cry—is the first real sacrifice I have to make for this excursion into solitude. I step out onto the deck and survey the big ridge the lower house looks out upon. One of the former residents named it Rattlesnake Ridge after he rode his bicycle up there and saw a bunch of rattlesnakes. The air cool and misty, the light fast fading, I spot one tree on the ridge that stands apart from the rest and take up my binoculars for a closer look. The tree is a huge Douglas fir, and maybe because of where it's perched, the wind has ripped a swatch from its midsection.

That night, my father and I sit down to a dinner of pork chops fried in a cast iron skillet, homemade biscuits, applesauce. We light the wall lamps, bank the fire, do dishes. Small things to keep busy, to keep sadness at bay. Before bed, I slip out onto the deck in my shirtsleeves one last time and stare for a moment into the dark. My mother is all alone, my grandmother is gone, and out on Rattlesnake Ridge is a tree with a hole in it.

THOUGH WE ARE BOTH SADDENED by the loss of my grandmother, our next four days together are good days. Mild days. Slow. Deliberate. My father works hard on the mowing and has the pond area looking like a park. I rototill the garden, weed the strawberries, split and stack kindling for the stove. In a tool shed we discover pans for panning gold and give it a shot. But that's mostly my father. I'm content to practice my fly cast, to scrabble about on the rocks, looking around, taking my bearings. In the weeds not far from the unmarked trail to the homestead are what look like huge sections of rusty stovepipe, the remains of a mining operation. Bradley explained to me the techniques the miners employed. They set up these pipes at springs and creeks high on the mountain, and the pipes fed hoses called giants that were used to blast the topsoil away, down into sluice boxes, where it could be sifted and searched through. Over time much earth was displaced, the hillsides gouged and scraped out.

When we'd first come down here, I'd thought of these gulches and draws as natural, as the result of flooding and erosion, not as man-made scars on the land. My father still doesn't see it that way. Down on his knees at the river's edge, using a pair of tweezers to pick through the sand in his mining pan, dropping flecks of gold into a glass vial, he imagines what a gold nugget could buy.

One day on our hike back to the cabin he says it's too bad gold can't be picked up with a magnet, otherwise we'd come down here and make ourselves a fortune. If gold could be extracted with a magnet, I respond, the Rogue River would be neither wild nor scenic.

And though I love my father and am grateful for our time

together, conversations like this (and like the one we had about taking back reservation land from Native Americans) make me crazy. Pair this with the anxiety I'm feeling about living here by myself, and tensions that ordinarily would get left alone suddenly flare up. One day I yell at him about slurping his beef stew. Another time, as we're walking the rototiller back to the barn after having tilled the garden, he takes the handle of a garden rake and tries to knock the clumped mud off my boots. "What in the hell do you think you're doing?" I demand.

"Just helping you—"

"You can't always *help* me."

I don't know whether he understands the extent to which my mood is the product of fear and anxiety. He doesn't show signs of being hurt by what I've said, but we never really show emotion. So who knows?

These moments aside, however, my father and I get along well enough. When we talk it's usually about simple things: what's for lunch, what we've seen along the trails, what we've read in a book. We tell a few favorite stories about my late grandmother, our private memorial service to her. By the end of the week, he's ready to go home, and I'm ready for him to go home.

On the day of his departure—Good Friday—we're up at first light, lugging his suitcase two miles up the homestead's driveway. In a fitting symmetry to the day of our arrival, the cold has returned, and it's decided to snow. Big feathery flakes that somehow make the quiet of the forest seem even quieter. Pausing every so often to catch our breath, to set down the suitcase and rest a moment, I swear I can hear the soft puff of individual snowflakes hitting the papery-skinned madrones along the road. Such moments make the cold, wet climb up the driveway with a heavy suitcase worth it. And if it's not too odd to say, the sight of my truck at the top of the drive—parked right where we left it, not a shotgun shell in sight—feels like a blessing, a kind of salvation.

When I insert the key and turn it, the engine fires right up.

On our way out of the homestead, we bump east along the BLM road, stunning views opening up before us that on the drive in last week had been obscured by cloud cover: miles and miles of backcountry mountains, some of it gorgeous forest and some of it the slash and burn of a timber operation. The farther we get from the homestead, the more the road improves. From hard-packed clay to loose gravel, gravel to patchy asphalt, patchy asphalt to a smooth two-lane highway with painted yellow lines. Toward town the road follows the river, its glassy green waters. And a farm or two appear, big open acreages with horses cropping grass in the pastures, a few fat black cattle.

In the village of Merlin there is an elementary school, a gas station, several local home-style restaurants with a couple cars apiece in their parking lots. A sixties-era VW van on the side of the road advertises GIANT CINNAMON ROLLS. Bradley told me about a fly shop in Merlin called The Silver Sedge. Past residents have gone to its owner for flies and advice, but I'm still too green. I really wouldn't know what to do with some sage fly fisherman's advice. Maybe I'll see him in the fall.

Down the interstate in Grants Pass, my father and I take a room at the same hotel we stayed at last week, eat lunch at the same restaurant. Then we're off to find snow tires and chains. At the tire place—Big O Tires—I'm shown how to put on the snow chains and told that if I don't end up using them I can return them for a full refund once the threat of snow has passed. Because they are so friendly, I don't think they're trying to rip me off when one of the men changing my tires informs me that he did a brake inspection and my brakes are shot. So I get a brake job. My father and I slip across the street to Dairy Queen. It's the hour of school letting out, and we're soon joined by throngs of noisy high schoolers, fresh-faced boys and girls laughing and goofing off. The kind mechanics, these wholesome kids—is it possible we've gone back in time to the fifties? Or has Grants Pass, Oregon, never changed? My father and I watch the kids with their ice cream. He doesn't say so, but I know what he's thinking: once upon a time, that was him, just a kid with an ice cream cone. Moments like these, I miss him already.

THE FOLLOWING MORNING, I DRIVE my father to the bus station at six o'clock. He's taking the Greyhound from Grants Pass to Portland, where he'll catch an Amtrak and book a sleeper car home. He doesn't like to fly and won't unless he absolutely has to (i.e., my mother makes him). We sit in the truck until the bus arrives.

"Be careful," he says.

"I will."

When the bus pulls up, I get out and grab his suitcase from the back of the truck. He says good-bye and starts down the concrete platform. Then he stops, as though he's remembered something. He hugs me.

"From your mother."

"Okay," I say.

"Be careful," he says again.

After he has disappeared inside and his suitcase has been stowed, I give the bus a wave good-bye and stroll back to my truck. Simple as that, solitude begins. I drive away from the station and head west, giddy at my prospects. I've got my mud and snow tires, my chains, a month's worth of groceries and supplies. Forty-five miles down the road, a backcountry homestead waits with open arms.

The drive in, alone, everything is sunshine and mountains. I've got the radio cranked and am singing along. I'd thought that I would be scared, scared to death. But now that it's here, now that I'm actually facing the thing I'd been so afraid of, I am happy. Two hours pass in no time, and soon I'm turning down the drive, unlocking the upper gate, slipping through, then getting out again and locking it up behind me. Nothing to it. I slip down to the lower gate to repeat the procedure. Only the lower gate—once I've reached up into the gate box and slipped off the lock—won't budge. I push the metal bar, thinking maybe the tongue that the lock rests upon is stuck in its groove. Nothing. I bump it with my hips. Still nothing. I stand back, assess the problem, and the forest all around me gets eerily silent, as though waiting to see what I will do next. I bump the bar with my hips again, harder this time. The gate still won't budge. Not good. *Not good.* I think for a moment about nudging the gate with the nose of my truck, but I don't want to wreck the gate or ding my vehicle. Then I look around for a chunk of wood. If it's really a problem of loosing the lock's tongue from the gate box, then maybe a few whacks from something solid will encourage it. I find a hefty chunk of madrone, eye the bar where it enters the gate box, and pound it. On the fourth blow, my sledge splinters apart.

I sit on my front bumper, miserable, on the verge of tears. What the hell am I going to do now?

I'll have to hike down to the cabin and use the satellite phone to call Bradley for help. The feeling makes me sick. And what's Bradley supposed to do from Portland? That's nearly three hundred miles away.

I sit on the bumper, head in my hands. Then suddenly it hits me. No, I can't be this stupid. I leap up, scrabble to the gate box, and reach up into it, feeling around with my fingers. The pin! The goddamned pin! I took off the lock but failed to take off the pin the lock attached to.

Now I really am crying.

And laughing.

I push the pin, the gate springs open.

MY PRIDE HAVING DODGED A BULLET, there's nothing left to do but unload groceries, settle in, start a fire in the stove, and put my feet up. I drowse in the La-Z-Boy recliner, listen to the hiss and crackle of a couple sticks of madrone. As much as I pretend, however, I can't quite get comfortable. I skim a book or two, play my guitar. Midafternoon, in the middle of a letter to a friend, I decide for some reason to stop and look outside. Down in the garden, palming one of John Daniel's leftover purple cabbages like a basketball, sits a young black bear. On Frank's advice, I take a police whistle and creep onto the deck. From how he described it, a whistle should make this bear jump out of its skin. So I take a deep breath and blow a long, shrill, piercing note. The bear doesn't budge. It simply goes on dithering over John Daniel's cabbages, a shopper at market. I blow the whistle again. Harder. I shout and wave my arms: "Get out of here, bear! Git!" And finally, after I've raised a big-enough stink, the bear rolls its head my way and lazily squints up at me. Oh, it seems to say. Oh, okay. And it beats a slow retreat out of the garden, through the fence, and into the forest beyond. Later, feeling lonely and wishing I hadn't hurried my company off so quickly, I slip down to the garden. Wrapped tightly around one of the barbs on the barbed-wire fence, I find a big tuft of hair left there for me like a welcome gift. I untangle it from the metal barb. The hair is coarse and black, much coarser and blacker than I'd have guessed, judging from how glossily it shone in the sun.

4

VOCATION TO
SOLITUDE

ALREADY I LOVE THESE MORNINGS. No alarm clock, no boring job to rush off to, just the slow and steady coming-to-consciousness brought on by an almost imperceptibly lightening sky. Out on the deck in shirtsleeves, early, hugging myself against the chill, I watch huge flame-shaped wisps of fog rise from the river canyon and drift over the black backlit mountains. In the air is a whiff of smoke from the fire I let die out last night, the smoke mixing with the damp-earth smell of the valley. The day getting started. Possibilities. Down in the meadow a few deer browse in the long grass, looking up from time to time, twitching their ears. From the surrounding forest comes a variety of birdsong, and I listen for sounds I know and can identify: the cheep of robins, the maniacal laugh of pileated woodpeckers, the raspy screeching of Steller's jays. These are the few moments of the day—just standing here, watching, listening—before the motor of my mind begins to whir and click, cranking out its polluted thoughts of what I could or should be doing with this time, of what I might be missing back home, of all the bad things that could happen to a person this removed from civilization. These are the few moments of the day when I am perfectly, unequivocally happy. Waiting for the sun to come up.

Eventually, however, hunger pulls me inside, and I stoke the fire, fix something to eat, listen for a few minutes to the local NPR affiliate on my AM radio. Then I fire up my laptop and try for a few hours to write.

There is no electricity at the homestead save what comes from a gas generator, so to power my laptop—because, sadly, I haven't the patience or the will for a manual typewriter or to write by hand—I use a device a friend back home rigged up for me. Two heavy van batteries wired together in a hard-shell suitcase. The kind of device a terrorist in the movies might try to sneak onto an airplane. The battery pack gives me exactly enough juice to write two hours a day for about a week. On my weekly trips to town, I plug it into my truck's cigarette lighter to recharge.

After an hour or two of pecking away at the keyboard, describing the lives and struggles of the people of my imagination, trying to decipher the meaning of their pain, I start to lose focus, lose the ability to make a dream out of words, and have to stop for the day. I close my laptop, shake out my hands, look outside. The sun is full up now, the mountains are green, the deer have moved on to the rest of their morning. I should do the breakfast dishes lest Mr. Bear get interested in the smell. After that I should do some chores. Read a book. Something. Thoreau famously said he went to the woods because he "wished to live deliberately, to front only the essential facts of life, and see if I could not learn what it had to teach, and not, when I came to die, discover that I had not lived." I don't know if I'm that ambitious. I have two main goals: since this is a writing residency, I'll get up every morning and write; and after having written, I'll try to spend as much time outside as possible. This is my attitude for the time being. If seven months of this regimen instills in me something along the lines of what Thoreau set out to learn at Walden, wonderful. If not, then what have I lost?

Bradley's manual with its list of chores helps me accomplish the second of my two main goals. Every morning after I close my laptop and do the breakfast dishes, I flip through the manual and find a chore. This early in the spring, there is plenty of mowing. I mow firebreaks around the houses and down at the turnaround. I mow the tall grass under the apple trees in the garden. I mow the center strip down the rutted driveway (which Bradley said should be kept short lest it come into contact with the hot underside of my truck engine and somehow ignite). When I'm sick of the noise and exhaust of mowing, I grab a pair of loppers and start in on the reclamation project Bradley has assigned for me in the little meadow flanking the pond.

I work on my knees, lopping Douglas fir saplings and tossing them onto an ever-growing pile. A quiet, meditative, and brainless activity, it's the perfect antidote to a morning spent writing.

My third day at work on this task, something amazing happens. A series of heavy gray clouds rolls in, and it starts to snow. Soft and airy, the flakes meander to earth with a kind of feathery reluctance. They cling to the sleeves of my flannel shirt, my sock cap: a spring squall in a remote mountain meadow. To be alone here, the snow flying sideways in dizzying patterns against the canopy of Douglas firs and madrones, making rings on the surface of the pond. To hear the barred owls start hooting, one and then another, and then another still, their staccato barks like a pack of dogs on a winter's night. An owl calls from a Douglas fir not twenty-five feet over my head. I look up, blinking against

45

the snow, and there it sits on a dead limb, its delicate geishalike face scanning the forest, the tiny soft-looking brown feathers on its chest aflutter in the breeze.

Back at the cabin at lunchtime, getting a fire going in the stove, heating up beef stew, I think about the snowy sky, the meadow, how it felt to witness that fleeting moment. Later I grab my backpack and head to the river in search of more moments to witness. Sometimes I bring my fly rod and spend an hour casting, catching nothing. Other times I leave the rod behind in favor of binoculars, a camera. Landmarks are becoming familiar—the gold miners' rusting pipes, certain oddly shaped rocks at the river, a burned-up stump I always mistake for a bear. Day in and day out, quietly walking the homestead's sun-dappled trails, I half expect to be attacked. Only it never happens, and it almost disappoints me that it never happens. On one hand, if the bears—like the bears of my dreams last winter—are going to kill me, I wish they'd hurry up and get it over with already. On the other hand, lacking human companionship as I do, the thought of seeing a bear—like the one I saw in the garden—staves off loneliness.

Not that I am doing too badly on the loneliness front. Back at the cabin at the end of the day, sitting in the rocker on the deck and looking out at Rattlesnake Ridge, at the tree with the hole in it, I don't really feel alone. I've got my people—my mother and father, my friends, my grandmother who recently passed away. I can almost hear their voices, old conversations, as though being alone out here has somehow brought them closer to me. The need for them has brought them closer. On these afternoons, thinking of my people, I reflect on all the happy and not-so-happy accidents that led me to the homestead, that made me want to become a writer in the first place. Like the death of my paternal grandmother some sixteen years ago. After she died the family—my father's brother and sisters, their spouses and children—set about cleaning out her house, salvaging what could be salvaged and divvying up what could be divvied up. Having come from nothing—a girlhood on a farm in southern Illinois at the height of the Great Depression—my grandmother didn't have much of real value, but in a back closet, wrapped in a white handkerchief, someone found my late grandfather's Colt .32 service revolver. He'd been a marine between world wars, had served in Australia and China, and died just three weeks to the day after I was born. The gun was fabulous, easily the day's best find. Black, beat up, old looking, it radiated a sense of danger and intrigue. It had stories to tell.

My brother and I weren't allowed to play with it, of course, and in my dejection over that I gave up searching the house. There wasn't going to be anything better found. The whole enterprise was depressing. My grandmother—who could hug like no one else—was gone and wasn't ever coming back. Likewise, I knew I wouldn't be coming back to her little white house in Effingham, Illinois.

One of my aunts must have noticed and thought that I needed something to keep busy. Or maybe it was my mother.

I was given a handful of photocopied pages from my grand-mother's diary, written not long after I was born. They had been typed up by one of my aunts, and most entries began with an apology for it having been so long since the last time she had written. Though I wasn't a big reader, these pages captivated me. They told of her childhood, her mischief and its consequences; of seeing her brother off at the train station when he left for World War I; of the colorful backwoods neighbors she knew in the Illinois of the 1920s and '30s. But more than that: as I sat there in her kitchen reading, oblivious to the work going on around me—the work of disassembling her life—I heard her voice rising up off the page. Her rich, familiar, raspy voice.

That encounter with language and feeling, more so than any other, made me want to write. The diary entries were my first lesson in storytelling. From them I learned that, told well, a story could indeed raise the dead.

In that spirit I get up every morning and write. I do my chores, take hikes, and try to be mindful of what I have seen, felt, and thought. In letters home, which I type at night under the flickering glow of propane wall lamps, I savor my new vocabulary, words like *fence lizard, black bear, rough-skinned newt*. In so doing I become aware of what's underneath the words, what gives them their shape: the soft sound of black-tailed deer wading through blackberry canes at dawn; bats scratching to life at dusk under the cedar shakes of the upper house; the squeaky groan of the driveway gate when it swings open on my way to town, and the sound when it swings closed upon my return; water purling from a PVC pipe at the pond; the river gnashing its teeth on the rapids; mice skittering in the breezeway; the sound of my own voice.

Yet if I am being honest I have to admit that no matter how heavily I stuff my days with chores, reading, or remembering, no matter how closely I cleave to the simple program I've set out for myself of writing and spending time outside, there is always an hour or two at night, and often it's longer, that is beyond my ability to fill. An hour or two when loneliness is a bitter taste in my mouth.

Nights it gets bad, I suffer insomnia and take out my frustration on the mice. The back bedroom shares a wall with the breezeway, and I can hear them skittering around, squeaking.

I pound the walls and scream at them: "Shut up, shut up, shut up!" I hoot like the barred owls I've heard, thinking it might scare them.

Still, it's not the mice keeping me awake—it's my own mind. After I've prepared and eaten my dinner; after I've washed a sink full of dishes, dried them, and put them away; after I've set aside whatever book I've lost myself in; after I've switched off the propane wall lamps and the mantels are glowing, cooling; after I've slipped out onto the deck for one last look at Rattlesnake Ridge under its twinkling star fields; after I've undressed and climbed into bed, my mind comes alive with questions: Why the owl? Why the newt? Why snow on a Douglas fir? Why the river? Why the sound of the river—from far away, from up close? Why the sky for birds to fly through, to fall through? Why the stars so far away? Why loneliness? Why happiness? Why emptiness that won't be filled but so easily fills me? Why red rust on the garden gate? Why the tree with the hole in it? Why tiny orange lichens? Lying in bed at the end of the day—mice scrabbling in the walls behind my headboard—the questions gape open like a second night sky with its own stars, constellations, and legends.

AT THE END OF THE WEEK—after six days alone—I haul my laundry out to the truck and set off for town, eager for proof that I'm not the last living soul on Earth. Things that I never thought I'd miss, like highways swarming with cars, like stop signs, scraps of trash along the roadside: I miss them. And I'm eager to see people, strangers even. To see that life has gone on while I've been away. Mostly, though, I just want to make some phone calls home and to check my new mailbox for letters. Six days alone and you know who loves you and what love means.

The drive to town is a beautiful one, the remote logging roads offering expansive views of the forest and the river, all of it blanketed with fog. I stop a few times, get out, breathe in the morning coolness, savor the quiet. Even sections of clear-cut forest—even they seem beautiful on the way to town.

In Grants Pass my first order of business is to stop by the post office and collect any mail that has floated my way. To be able to carry home with me the voices of friends and family, to hear the news from them, to catch up, to know I've not been forgotten out here on the West Coast—the feeling is priceless. And after a week alone, after this two-hour commute to town, it takes every bit of restraint I can muster not to rip the letters open and read them on the spot. But since I want to save them for the lonely hours back at the homestead, I somehow manage it. Then it's off to the Laundromat, where again I have to resist the urge to read the letters while waiting for my laundry to finish rinsing and drying. What keeps me honest here is that I'm only a half hour from phone calls. I make these at the grocery store, where there is a bank of pay phones. I call my folks, and we talk for a while about my father's return trip to Indiana, and about my grandmother's funeral service. "Have you thought any more about Granny's van?" I ask my mother.

"Not yet," my mother says.

"Okay," I say.

"Everything's still too up in the air."

The van is my grandmother's minivan—a white GMC Safari with green stripes. I'd been driving it back in December before I bought my truck, and my friend Michelle, who'd just found out that she was pregnant, said it was the kind of vehicle she was going to need if she had a kid. The car she drives now is a rusty '81 Mercury without an exhaust pipe. She hasn't the money for anything better.

Since both my parents already had vehicles—nice ones, at that—it occurred to me that we could give Michelle the van.

So far, however, my mother isn't biting. Not that I blame her, and not that I push the issue. It's an emotional time. It's not easy being the executrix of a will, trying to be fair and transparent with a sister in far-off Houston, deciphering the actual value of bank accounts, investments, property. Still, I figure it can't hurt to ask. No baby should have to ride around in the back of an exhaust-filled car.

After talking with my folks, I make a few more calls—to Michelle, to my friend Big Aaron—and then I buy some groceries and start the two-hour trip back to the homestead. West of the village of Merlin traffic drops off, and it's just the road, the river, the skyward-straining trees. It was nice to come to town and talk to everyone, and it's nice to return to solitude. I crank the radio, follow my BLM road numbers, snake around the mountains. Before I know it, I'm standing at the homestead's upper gate, fiddling with keys, unfastening the lock and pin, and passing through. Then it's the lower gate, where I had so much trouble on my first solo entry. Today it goes just fine, and I have to laugh at myself, thinking back on how I'd sunk my head into my hands, tears in my eyes. Was that really me? Down at the house, happy and exhausted after the daylong trip, I put away my groceries, plunk down in a rocking chair on the deck with the letters from my mailbox, and one by one, with a truly grateful heart, read them.

LATE IN APRIL THE RAIN all but stops, the temp begins to climb, and the days bleed one into the next. Every morning and evening the same three deer come down to the salt block, two yearling bucks with velvety nubs for antlers and a runt I name Cougar-Bait. The bigger ones pick on him, prod him with their hooves, try to run him off. He ducks under the split-rail fence for a quick getaway but soon is back, nibbling grass nearby, trying to come off as inconspicuous. Their adolescent playfulness is matched only by the vigilance with which they watch for predators. At the slightest sound they tense up, their mulish ears scanning the forest. They come in the morning when I'm writing and again in the evening after I've returned from chores or a hike. They slip out of the woods, cast sweeping glances all around, and saunter across the drive.

At the end of a long day—when the writing hasn't gone too well, or when I'm just tired and stiff from the day's chores—the deer are a welcome sight. They have become my friends.

But all this solitude in a wild place is starting to do something to me, my psyche, for which I hardly have the words. For example, another of the days I spent lopping saplings at the pond. As I worked along, I happened to glance down and see what looked like a cigarette butt in the grass, and somehow the sight of a piece of litter made my heart sing. I was so glad to see it there, in this supposedly pristine place. Then I realized that it wasn't a cigarette butt after all—it was just the nub from one of the cut saplings come loose from its sheath of bark. And I was devastated. On some level, I wanted this place to be spoiled so it better resembled the world I came from.

The world I knew.

For help understanding my confused mind and spirit, I turn to a book John Daniel bequeathed the homestead's library: *Thoughts in Solitude* by Thomas Merton. I copy long passages in a notebook to memorize.

> When we receive our solitude by intervals, we taste its value by contrast with another value. When we really live alone, there is no contrast.

> In disposing ourselves for this we need not attempt, by ourselves, the vain task of emptying ourselves of every image: we must first begin by replacing the harmful images with the good ones, then by renouncing even our good images that are useless or which involve us uselessly in passion and emotion. Landscape is a good liberator from all such images, for it calms and pacifies the imagination and the emotions and leaves the will free to seek God.

> Suppose that by pretending to empty myself, pretending to be silent, I am really trying to cajole God into enriching me with some experience—what then?

> Vocation to Solitude—to deliver oneself up, to hand oneself over, entrust oneself completely to the silence of a wide landscape of woods and hills, or sea, or desert; to sit still while the

sun comes up over that land and fills its silences with light. To pray and work in the morning and labor and rest in the afternoon, and to sit still again in meditation in the evening when night falls upon the land and when the silence fills itself with darkness and with stars. This is a true and special vocation. There are few who are willing to belong completely to such silence, to let it soak into their bones, to breathe nothing but silence, to feed on silence, and to turn the very substance of their life into a living and vigilant silence.

We may indeed look ahead and foresee and desire the path that leads us to the desert, but in the end, solitaries are made by God and not by man.

Is it God who wakes me from a dream one night near the end of my first month alone and has me stumble onto the deck, bleary eyed, to look at the stars? Deep in the river canyon, surrounded on all sides by the rugged, sprawling Klamath Mountains, the starshine spills in unimpeded. I'm watching the stars, feeling as though I've woken from a dream into a dream—stars that blink red and blue, that burn bright white, that streak and flare out—when suddenly, up on Rattlesnake Ridge, the horizon begins to lighten. It takes me a moment to realize: It's a spaceship! No, it's the full moon!

Enormous, luminous, the moonrise shoots wide white beams across the mountain. The barn roof comes into relief, each cedar shake. My friends the deer stand still a moment in the meadow behind the garden, as though spooked by the sudden appearance of their shadows. I am awestruck, stupefied. The moon pulses like a white-hot heart through the exposed rib cage of the tree with the hole in it.

Two thousand miles east of the homestead, my friends and family back home are asleep under this same moon. And I am here. And the deer drifting across the meadow are here. And the coyotes yipping down at Horseshoe Bend are here. I listen for a moment to their shrill, almost human cries. Then I realize: they *are* human. Human voices yipping, howling, crying out—I hear them. And I hear drums, a steady beat. Pounding. Though I know that it's probably just rafters who've brought their drums with them from Grants Pass or wherever they've come from, a part of me can't help but imagine that it's the river's original inhabitants, the Rogue River Indian peoples, dancing, singing, pounding drums. Or maybe it's their angry ghosts pounding the skulls of the whites who murdered them. I want so badly to sing and howl along, to add my small voice to theirs. But for now I've been called to solitude. Silence is my howling.

Vocation to Solitude

5

SPRING VISITORS

SOME MORNINGS IN LATE APRIL IT'S still cool enough that I start a little fire in the stove. Others I forgo a fire and sit in the sun at my writing table, rubbing my hands, blowing on them. "Time is about to slow way down for you," a friend of mine writes in a letter, and she is correct. I measure time by the strawberries in the garden. When I arrived, they were beginning to blossom. Now they sport tiny fruits.

All that keeps me tethered to the human timescale is the digital clock John Daniel left behind and my calendar on the wall. I flip ahead, May, June, July, counting the days I'll spend here alone. Two hundred ten.

In my more immediate future I've got a series of visitors to prepare for: Bradley and his two young kids, my folks, my brother and his wife, and a man named Dave Reed from the Medford Bureau of Land Management. After the past few weeks of having no one to talk to but the deer, I'm eager for company. Yet at the same time, I realize that the moment someone else arrives at the homestead—even if it's someone I love, like my mother—I lose something. I become the me of before, whom everybody already knows, and the new person I'm cultivating goes dormant inside. If I were a more devout hermit this would probably bother me. But I can't help it: I miss people. To hell with spiritual enlightenment.

The first visitors to arrive and relieve me of my solitude are Bradley and his kids. Midafternoon on a Friday, the last weekend of April, I hear the shudder of a truck engine switching off at the upper house. An hour later, here they come, bouncing down the driveway in Bradley's pickup. They park at the bottom of the turnaround, and I go down and greet them. The kids are both dark-haired with dimples.

Hollynd is seven, Wilder five. They grin and fidget and hang close to their dad, who's rooting around the bed of his truck for his fly rod and his creel. "Look at this," Bradley says to me, tickled, holding up a pair of the smallest-looking fly rods I've ever seen. "They're the perfect size. Oh, I can't wait, man. I can't wait to see them cast these things." He invites me along on their fishing trip, and after another few minutes of gearing up, we start down the trail to the river. And right away I learn something: with Bradley and his kids in it, the forest is a different place. They bring it back to scale somehow, give the forest a manageable proportion. Rather than ominous and silent—the way I've known it—the forest is a wonderland, filled with warmth and sunlight and the sweet sound of Wilder's and Hollynd's laughter.

The two of them are incredibly curious. Every so often they stop and kneel down to investigate a bug or a wildflower, studying it intensely, as though their lives hang in the balance. Then, just as suddenly, they pop up and scamper down the trail after their father. At the river, Wilder scrabbles across the big rocks to keep up. At crevasses that for Bradley and me are little more than a single stride, a hop and a skip for Hollynd, Wilder has to leap to get across. Perched on the edge of the rock, he repeats a mantra under his breath: "I can do it! I can do it!" And he leaps.

Bradley sets them both up with rods and flies and gets them started casting with the same lesson he'd given me a few weeks back. The kids take to it more quickly than I did and are soon waving their fly rods like pros, their lines shooting out in ten-foot arcs. Bradley and I stand back and watch.

"To be able to come down here with them," Bradley says, shaking his head, amazed. "What a gift."

I can only imagine what it must feel like for Bradley to share this place, and his boyhood memories of this place, with his kids. To be able to pass on to them something of his feeling for the rocks and trees, for the sound of the river, the flash of a steelhead. And I have to admit: it is a gift, all of it. I feel lucky to stand here. Over the past several years—a cynical holdover from my divorce perhaps—I've stopped believing in the basic goodness of this life. I have tended to look at the good memories from my own childhood as little more than moments of pitiable ignorance, moments I didn't know any better than to be happy. But here, in the form of these kids fishing with their father as I fished with my father, in the form of this wild green river charging westward through the mountains: Here is incontrovertible evidence to the contrary. Here is the good.

Back at the cabin that evening, Bradley invites me for dinner: barbecued chicken, guacamole, a pan full of spuds. The kids sit coloring at the table. It's such a banal scene that I hardly know what to make of its power: a father cooking dinner, two children happily at work with their crayons. I slip onto the deck, look out at ten misty miles of river canyon, mountain-on-mountain gray in the dusk.

"What a gift," Bradley says again.

"What a gift," I say.

Later still, the kids in bed, asleep, Bradley and I sip Beam on ice under the stars. He tells me stories: the time someone accidentally killed a bear in one of the fruit trees with a .22 rifle; the time he hooked the bridge of his nose with a fly he was casting. In the dark, a drink in hand, the stories wash over me.

When it's finally time to go I'm the proverbial three sheets to the wind and realize I've forgotten to bring a flashlight for the quarter-mile walk home in the dark. Bradley is kind enough to set me up with a kerosene lantern. With the weather as dry as it's been—middle of a ten-year drought, he reminds me—I'm to be especially careful with the lantern's open flame. In these conditions the smallest mishap or bit of carelessness could prove disastrous. On the way out the door, I shake his hand and thank him, try my best to articulate all the goodness I feel here. He nods. He knows. I walk the road home, drunk, daintily carrying a lantern between my forefinger and thumb.

MID-MAY MY FOLKS FLY IN TO Portland with my eighty-four-year-old adopted grandfather, Maurice, rent an SUV, and burn some 270 miles down I-5 to Grants Pass, where I meet them at a gas station. My mother, having spent the past two years taking care of her dying mother, looks more rested and at peace than I have seen her in a long time. My father is my father, sunglasses on a cord around his neck. Maurice, who lived with his own parents until they died, who never married, who became my grandmother's companion only after they'd danced together for several years on the senior circuit in Vandalia, Illinois, has the look of a man hollowed out by grief. His watery blue eyes look past the trees and the highway, beyond anything the rest of us can see. He loved my grandmother and lost her. The loneliness of my days out here is nothing compared to his.

Spring Visitors

We spend the night at the Motel 6 in Grants Pass and drive into the homestead the next morning. My poor mother—I make her ride in the truck with me and talk her ear off. I tell her about the bear I saw in the garden, about the tuft of its hair in the fence. I tell her about Bradley and his kids. It's a blazingly hot day, and the mountains radiate heat in blurry waves. Turkey vultures sail high above it all.

At the homestead we bump our way down the drive and at the upper house get out to take in the view of the river canyon. My mother says it's beautiful. My father says it looked a lot different a month and a half ago. Maurice looks around approvingly, asks if I have a garden. "Not yet," I say. "I'm slow."

"We could plant you one while we're here," my mother says, looking around at the upper house and down at the old orchard below. "You have any seeds with you?" she says. Then, "Gosh, it really is quiet."

We spend the day messing around—I show them the old barn and the garden, take them up to the pond, and use a long-handled pool skimmer to fish out a handful of rough-skinned newts. They are soft and wiggly and never to be licked, Bradley told me, because their skins are incredibly toxic. So we just hold them, turn them over in our hands, stroke their orange bellies. Then it's on to lunch and the rest of the afternoon, which we spend in the shade of the deck at the lower house, waiting out the heat. My father tells Maurice that when we were here earlier in the spring I sent him out every morning to get eaten by the bears. "And what did I have for protection?"

"What?"

"A hammer handle."

"Just the handle?" Maurice says.

"Bear could've used it to tenderize him," my mother says, laughing and poking my father in the ribs. "Tough old man needs it."

Once the sun's gone down and it's started to cool off, we start dinner and make a plan for tomorrow. Since neither my mother nor Maurice is physically able to get down to the river and back (the trail is just too steep), I suggest that we all pile into their rented suv and head to the coast at Gold Beach. I've been wanting to go anyway, to see what's out there, and—if nothing else—it'll be cooler.

So the next morning, after quickly helping me plant a modest garden of sweet corn and sugar snap peas, my folks and Maurice and I hit the road, heading west. We don't have a map but take it on faith that these backcountry logging roads have to lead somewhere. Along the way, the scenery is gorgeous: rugged mountains and forest, tiny shining creeks burbling over craggy-faced boulders. After two and a half, three hours, we emerge from the logging road onto a paved highway flanked on either side by tidal estuaries reminiscent of the drainage ditches alongside roads back home in Indiana. We come to a big bridge and a view of the ocean, its stunning blue flatness. The size of it dwarfs the solitary walkers far down the beach and the kite flyers with their high-flying rainbow kites. We cruise the main drag in Gold Beach, cross over the wide mouth of the Rogue, and find a reasonably priced hotel on the water.

Three days of rest and relaxation in a resort town. That's our plan for the week. Yet as good as it feels to be surrounded by family, and as much as I've missed them in the past month and a half, a nagging anxiety hangs over me: I've not come to Oregon to be here with anyone else; I've come to be alone.

The anxiety, I suppose, stems from my fear of losing the gains I've made so far. The painful adjustments. How to do without people, their constant reassuring presence. How to do without daily conversation.

Hard lessons.

I'd rather not repeat them.

Spring Visitors

So over the next three days, while I try to make the best of my time with Maurice and my folks, my mind is often elsewhere. We eat dinner at a Chinese restaurant or watch television in the hotel (the wind having whipped up a sandstorm on the beach), and I start thinking about the three deer who hang around the lower cabin, Cougar-Bait and his friends. I wonder whether the bear has broken into the garden again. (After Bradley's last visit, during which he set up his bear licks, baiting them with peanut butter, I've been expecting fireworks, but nothing's happened. The peanut butter hasn't been touched.) These details and a thousand others swim through my mind like so many toxic rough-skinned newts. Thankfully, my family is happy-go-lucky. They are content with touristy pleasures, like a jet-boat ride fifty miles up the Rogue for lunch at a wilderness lodge. Like driving around aimlessly, taking in the landscape. And more than that—they are good-spirited, funny, companionable. On our way back to the homestead at the end of the week, we stop in the middle of the Siskiyou National Forest, not a soul around for miles, so Maurice can drain his bladder. He asks if this is federal land. He and I are both Democrats, and my folks are staunch Republicans. I tell him it's federal land. He raises his fuzzy eyebrows, chuckles, and—loud enough for my folks to hear—says that if this is federal land then, by God, he's taking a piss on George W. Bush.

THE FIRST WEEK OF JUNE it's Dave Reed from the Medford branch of the Bureau of Land Management—a family friend of the Boydens—come to make sure the homestead's in shape for the upcoming fire season. He arrives bearing gifts: a pouch of Bear Creek soup, a fresh cantaloupe, and a loaf of cinnamon bread from a local bakery. Tall and lanky in his uniform, silver hair trimmed close about his ears, a tickled grin on his face as he hands over his gifts and introduces himself, Dave immediately strikes me as the picture of an outdoorsman kept too long indoors. On the deck with glasses of ice water, we chat, and he quizzes me about my background—where I'm from, what I do, what I think of the homestead and the Boydens and the river. He says he spent some time in Indiana in the army, and he tells me about his history with the Boyden family and how Bradley's father was the doctor who delivered him, sixty-some years ago, in a little hospital up in Astoria, Oregon. And he tells me about how some of the homestead's former residents—he won't name names—didn't at first blush seem up to the task of living here. He had worried about them, if they were prepared for the wilderness, the solitude.

After our brief visit, we walk the perimeter of the houses. Dave isn't impressed by my mowing. The grass is too long, won't stop a fire. Since he's been so friendly and has come with gifts, I resist the urge to tell him I put off cutting it this afternoon in order to meet him.

Instead, I say I'll do it first thing tomorrow. "Scout's honor," I say, holding up two fingers.

"First thing," Dave says.

Then he takes me up to the million-dollar pot patch a former caretaker (before the writing residency) had allegedly maintained. Hidden off the driveway a quarter mile, not far from the lower gate, sit several black cisterns and a broken television, a rusting television antenna, coils of hoses, and dozens of big mounds of earth that in the absence of cannabis have been reclaimed by fiddlehead ferns.

Apparently, the pot patch's overseer got greedy and cut down too many trees to let in the sunlight, making it easier for police helicopters to spot the plants. I look around at the junk left here to rot. It reminds me of the gold miners' rusting pipes down at the river, the timber slash of the clear-cuts I see from the road on my way to town. You can't exploit a place without leaving your mark. Yet I find it ironic that police helicopters are used for ferreting out a few pot plants when so many other crimes, especially crimes against the environment, exist in plain sight. Like those clear-cuts.

On the way back to his vehicle, Dave asks if any of my family or friends are set to visit, and I tell him that my brother and sister-in-law are due in a week. "You ought to take them to Crater Lake," Dave says.

"Yeah?"

"If you wanted," he says, "my wife and I'd even put you up for the night. You could drive in the next morning."

First the gifts of food, and now this invitation—to a stranger, to three strangers—to come spend the night. I'm unaccustomed to this kind of generosity and kindness, and coming as it does on the heels of a month alone, I am grateful beyond words. I wish I could take him up on it.

Unfortunately, however, my brother and sister-in-law are just passing through, en route to San Francisco on a road trip down the coast from Portland to San Diego. They'll only spend two nights at the homestead before taking off again. I tell Dave that another buddy of mine is thinking about coming out in August, and maybe I'll take him to Crater Lake by way of Medford, if the offer still stands. Dave says he and his wife would love to have us, says we won't be sorry about a trip to Crater Lake. "Bluest water you've ever seen," he says. Then he shakes my hand, hops into his truck, and fires up the engine. Before pulling away, he reminds me once more to cut that grass tomorrow. I promise him I will, I will. Up the road he goes with a wave, a tap of the horn.

THEY FLICKER BY, THESE VISITS. In the meantime—in the week or ten days between them—I work my system of writing, chores, and taking hikes. I look for my salvation, as a friend says in a letter, at the end of a hoe handle. Insight comes in tantalizing flashes. Returning to the cabin one day, carrying a few ripe strawberries from the garden, I see a banana slug sliming its way across a flat rock. It occurs to me that the banana slug might like to eat a strawberry. I set one down in front of it, big, juicy, and red. Thinking I'm here to kill it, however, the slug shrinks into a ball. So I back off, wait. After a moment there's a twittering of its tentacles, and its banana-peel body slowly investigates the strawberry. Over the next hour or two, as I come and go from the cabin, I check on the slug's progress. For having such small mouth parts it makes good time devouring a chunk of the berry. The insight is that you can be sliming around, minding your own business, when suddenly a strawberry appears. The insight is that this story happens. The insight is that this is exactly what Bradley and Frank have done for me—lain the gift of the homestead at my feet. Down on hands and knees watching the banana slug gum its way through the strawberry's tender, seeded flesh—something I'd never before thought to do—I realize that every day I'm alone is a blessing and a miracle. This is the insight.

Back before Bradley and the kids came, before my folks and Dave Reed—back during that first month I spent here by myself, when spring was still sloughing off winter and I was learning how to be alone—I missed people terribly, missed conversation, a sense of belonging to a community. I missed these things and felt as though my time here in Oregon were going to be an endurance test, a breath I held for seven months. I thought life here was a dream I'd someday wake up from, refreshed. But what I realize now that I've become better acquainted with the homestead, and with myself, is that it's the other way around: these people who visit are the dreams, and when I wake up it's to the reality of my solitude. While I host my visitors the homestead waits for me, and once everyone is gone it welcomes me home.

I said before that I judge time by strawberries down in the garden. Now I see my mistake: the strawberries are only ever themselves, growing and changing; time is the story I tell about their growing and changing.

Spring Visitors

In solitude, at a place like the homestead, the story of time's passing isn't nearly as interesting as the strawberry itself.

Or the slug.

So when visitors come it's they who are the dream, appearing and vanishing in astonishingly vivid interludes, leaving behind only the memory of their presence like dew in the grass. Bradley and his kids picking their way down the trail to the river, the forest quiet all around them. My mother and father and Maurice staring out at the ocean in Gold Beach. Dave Reed tapping his horn and driving up the road. There they go, one by one, leaving me alone here with the miracle of solitude.

With my brother and sister-in-law, their stay at the homestead is so brief it blurs like something glimpsed out a car window. I take them down through the big meadow to the river, and we spend a morning scrabbling on the rocks, exploring. In the afternoon my sister-in-law and I pick a big bowl of sour-pie cherries and make a pie while my brother strums my guitar on the deck. Bradley is here, too, come to see if he can't somehow raise the level of the pond, which Dave Reed says is way too low and in danger of sinking below the level of the pipe to the garden (something I should have been paying better attention to). We invite Bradley down for dinner, and I make a batch of pesto from a packet and drizzle it over pasta, shredded chicken, a couple of sliced red bell peppers. Around the dinner table Bradley is in rare form, telling us stories of Hathaway Jones, who used to deliver mail up and down the river by a team of mules. As he drove along he would make up tall tales about black bears and rattlers and watermelons. I look around at everyone's smiling faces, wishing this togetherness could last. It doesn't. It can't.

The next morning, I drive my brother and sister-in-law up the road to where they left their rental car and wish them good luck on the long drive south. That afternoon, Bradley and I sit on the deck of the lower house, talking for a few minutes before he too has to leave. "Solitude returns," Bradley says.

"So it does," I say.

"Dave Reed said you seemed lonely out here." Bradley is staring straight ahead at Rattlesnake Ridge. "You lonely?"

"Not really."

"No?"

"Not in a bad way."

Bradley nods, and we commiserate about how exactly a person living by himself two hours from town with no human contact is supposed to feel: wouldn't it be more troubling to know that someone didn't feel lonely? "You'd be a sociopath or something," Bradley says. "So you get lonely."

"So I get lonely," I say.

We're both quiet a second, and Bradley admits that the pond level is dangerously low, that that's the kind of thing I should call him about in the future. And I know he's right. I had seen the water going down, down, down, almost below the pipe, and didn't do anything about it. Just watched it. I tell him I won't hesitate to call him next time. Then he tells me the meadow looks good, the mowing I did. Everything's in great shape for the summer. He says if I want, I can start going around and digging out bull thistle, wherever I see it. I tell him that's good to know, because most of the chores listed in the manual are either for the spring or the fall, that there isn't much for the summer. Bradley looks at me a moment, a concerned look spreading across his face (a look not all that different from when he eyeballed my truck that first weekend), and I realize that I've said something wrong, that I have somehow offended Bradley's sense of propriety.

"You know," he says, "it doesn't have to be in the manual for you to do it. You're living here now. You own this place. Take ownership. If you see something that needs doing, just do it. You don't have to wait."

"Okay," I say.

"There's a stack of wood that needs splitting behind the shed. You could do that. You could take down the corral fence."

Spring Visitors

"Okay," I say again.

Bradley's still looking at me, chewing his bottom lip, as though wondering if anything he's said has gotten through. I'm looking out at Rattlesnake Ridge, at the tree with the hole in it. Down deep I know he's right—that taking ownership of this place is exactly what I should do, what I need to do—but I'm too stubborn and proud to admit that I don't know how. Instead, I just nod again, unconvincingly, and tell him I'll do my best—I'll dig up the thistles, split the wood, take down the fence.

Later that afternoon, after Bradley has left, I open a dresser drawer in the bedroom and discover a mouse nest inside. The mouse has swaddled up one of my washcloths and packed it with hundreds of white threads from a pair of frayed blue jeans. It's a remarkable feat of engineering every bit as miraculous as that slug with its strawberry. But the discovery, coming as it does on the heels of the talking-to Bradley gave me, feels somehow invasive. Outraged by this mouse in my house, I take the nest in my palm and fling it off the deck. Then I head to the breezeway, where high on a shelf, in a brown paper bag, lurks a product called Just One Bite. Rodent poison. I discovered it while investigating the cabin and its environs my first couple of weeks here, and at the time it seemed too harsh. I figured that as long as the mice stayed out of my way, we could coexist. Now they're in my way. I open the package and break off a chunk the size of a Snickers bar and set it on a shelf where I know they'll get it. That night, lying in bed, I hear the mice tussling over the bait. One grabs it with his tiny sesame-seed teeth and drags it to the left. Then another steals it and drags it to the right. On and on they go, all night long. Finally I fall asleep. In the morning the cabin is perfectly still.

6

OWNERSHIP

COUGAR-BAIT AND THE YEARLING BUCKS disappear when I have visitors. They're not afraid of human beings—they haven't been around us enough to have learned to be afraid. Maybe it's all our noise and commotion, or the strange smell of us, that keeps them away. Or maybe it's that when people are around I stop paying as much attention to the deer. Regardless, it feels good when I see them again on their way to the salt lick under the apple trees. In the last month, they have begun to sprout their velvety antlers, six-inch spikes the thickness of rhubarb stalks. Embarrassed about this development, they skulk around the homestead like touchy teenagers with bad haircuts.

The other day one of the bigger ones got zapped by Bradley's electric fence. He'd gotten interested in something inside—maybe the sugar snap peas my mother and I planted in May—and got a jolt to the nose. I saw him jump straight in the air, kick his heels, and tear off into the woods. Cougar-Bait and the others just looked up, curious, then looked all around, shrugged, and followed him.

When I went out to check on the fence later, I found it diddled. The electric wire was tangled around the barbed wire of the fence. Grounded, it had no zap. This was worse damage than any bear had yet done.

Much to Bradley's chagrin, I'd had to tell him when he'd come in last weekend that nothing had touched the licks we set out. The peanut butter had just moldered in its tin tray until finally it turned white and grew a fine coating of fuzz. We decided the fault lay with my brand of choice, the all-natural, nothing-but-peanuts variety, and that I should bait it with Peter Pan or some other chemically enhanced slurry of sugar and grease—something to get Mr. Bear's attention. So far I've held off reloading the licks. And now, seeing how the deer leaped up after being shocked, I'm not sure I want to reset the solar-electric wire. It seems unnecessarily cruel. Obviously, I don't want a deer or a bear in the garden, because they could destroy the fruit trees or hurt themselves. So in the end, eventually, I reset it, telling myself it's for their own good. The bear licks, however, I leave empty. Bradley said he wants me to take more ownership of the homestead, that I should act as though this place were my own. I don't zap the bears.

Other of my decisions around here are not so well thought out. One day I'm walking up the road with the weed eater, trimming the tall grass between the ruts so my truck engine doesn't inadvertently spark a fire when I drive to town. It's getting late in the afternoon, sunlight angling through the tops of Douglas fir and madrone. Up ahead I catch a glimpse of a young bear scurrying over the edge of the road and disappearing down a hillside. Weed eater in tow, I run after him.

Ownership

I want him to attack me, knock me over, bite me. I want to feel his furry black paws clawing my face and neck.

But by the time I get to where I'd last seen him, the bear is gone. It's only then I realize what I've really done. What if it had been a mother and a cub? What if it had attacked? I give up weed eating for the day and walk back to the cabin. It must be the solitude. It's getting to me.

On another afternoon I'm sitting in the garden, looking at all the apple trees and the hard green fruits beginning to sprout. A rare overcast day in June, the sky is light gray, temp in the midsixties. There's a smell of rain in the air, but it isn't raining. In the quiet of the garden, surrounded by apple trees and cherry trees, huge Concord grapevines, my sugar snap peas, my patch of Illini sweet corn, I feel so close to everything and only want to feel closer. I take off my clothes. I want to be chilled to the bone. Leaving everything in the garden, I walk up the homestead's driveway, past the upper house, past the lower gate, a ridiculous person, stark raving naked save steel-toed boots.

Above the lower gate the forest gets denser, darker. The trees creak and groan. Lizards scuttle in the rocks. From far off down the canyon I hear the deranged cackle of a pileated woodpecker, laughing at me. But I keep walking. I dare myself to keep walking. I think about the bears and cougars that could be after me. I think about being spotted by someone out here tending a pot patch like the one Dave Reed from the BLM showed me. Everything that scares me only makes me stronger. That's how I feel, at least, until a big wet limb from a nearby Douglas fir suddenly crashes to the forest floor. It was solid one moment—a pulpy black limb in the forest ahead of me—and the next it collapsed. I know that these Doug firs, in their quest for sunlight, drop limbs all the time. That if they didn't, they'd never make it. And I know that my irrational fear of everything wild on this homestead is a limb I need to drop if I'm to keep growing. But right now I'm naked and alone, and I've been scaring myself by thinking about bears, cougars, and drug dealers. I've not seen or talked to anyone in more than a week. That the limb dropped in front of me like this—it means that I'm in danger, that something bad is going to happen to me.

AFTER SIX OR SEVEN DAYS alone at the homestead, it's a relief to load up my laundry and letters and set off for town. I've fallen into a rhythm there: mail, laundry, phone calls, groceries, a burger and a Coke at McDonald's. People are starting to look familiar to me. I always see the same long-haired, braceleted, tattooed, headphone-wearing man playing his air guitar as he strolls down the sidewalk to wherever he's going. It's always the same unhappy-looking woman folding clothes and making change for people at the Laundromat. The same elderly, sweet grocery clerk, telling me to have a nice day. The same young Latina, no more than fifteen or sixteen years old, handing me my sack of grease at McDonald's. These people, though they don't know it any more than the deer or the lizards back at the homestead: they are my friends out here.

I look into the unhappy woman's blue eyes when she gives me my change for the washing machine and smile my deepest kindness and compassion. I chat with the grocery clerk about the weather, about her great-granddaughter whose baby picture she wears on a button on her green apron. With all the honest sincerity I can muster, I tell the Latina at the drive-through: thank you, thank you, thank you.

Despite my fears to the contrary, nothing bad is happening. In fact, living alone is making me a better person.

At the grocery store one day a man in a motorized wheelchair says, "Could you grab me four cans of tomato paste?" He looks like a Vietnam vet: goatee, leather vest, black gloves with the fingers snipped off.

Ownership

He points to a high shelf.

I grab the cans.

On my way out to the parking lot later, I see him again: he's driving this big beat-up van, a cigarette dangling from his lip. He's got the stereo cranked, a heavy-metal song. I'd felt pity for him earlier, that he'd had to ask me for help getting his tomato paste. But what the hell did I know? The guy's a badass.

The best part of these trips to town are the phone calls. After a week of silence, of hearing only my own voice (and, for a few minutes in the morning, the droning of NPR's talking heads), a conversation with my people—with my mother and father, my friend Michelle—is like a healing balm. I tell them about my week, what I've seen and done and how it's been. Then they tell me about their weeks, about what my brother and the rest of the family are up to, about developments around Indiana. The big story recently has been the execution of Timothy McVeigh, the Oklahoma City bomber. It happened a few hours to our south in Terre Haute. I tell my mother and father that the death penalty is George W. Bush's attempt to lower CO_2 emissions. They tell me McVeigh deserved to die. But regardless of any differences of political opinion, how grateful I am to have these people to call, week in and week out, to share my stories with: without them, and without a home beyond the homestead, insanity might not be something I joke about.

Still no word on my grandmother's minivan. Apparently, my father has been using it when he goes on his weekly fishing trips. He has a pickup truck with a camper top, a beautiful rig, but it only gets something like twelve miles a gallon, and with gas prices going up the minivan is just a better option.

"Have you seen the car Michelle drives?" I gently ask my mother. "It doesn't have an exhaust pipe."

She says that the van's Blue Book value is forty-five hundred dollars, and she's worked it out to give Michelle a gift of that much. I am amazed by her generosity and tell her so. "But I think she really needs the van," I say.

She says she's sorry, but they just can't do it right now. I say it's fine, it's fine, it's a wonderful thing that she's going to give her some money. That in itself is above and beyond the call of duty. Then we're quiet a few seconds. I change the subject, talk about how I used her piecrust recipe in the cherry pie I made for Mike and Jill and Bradley. After we've said our good-byes for the week, after I've slipped through the grocery store for my food and supplies, and after I've hit the McDonald's drive-through and started back to the homestead, I think: It really is generous of my mother to give Michelle some money. How many of the rest of us, in her shoes, would do the same?

I'VE BEEN THINKING ABOUT MOTHERS in the short story I've started writing. It began with an image that came to me out of a place memory. At the back edge of our property line along Wildcat Creek stands a mature honey locust whose trunk is thronged with clusters of six-inch-long thorns. The thorns are an effective deterrent against white-tailed deer who like to rub the velvet off their antlers on young saplings. The thorns detach from the tree trunk, like the stinger of a honeybee. And the tree survives.

One year my mother twisted thorns off by the handful and glue-gunned them into a crown of thorns for the altar at church.

Years later, a student of mine in a writing class at Purdue wrote an essay about how every Easter the women of her family would walk the woods behind her house and do the exact same thing—make a crown of thorns.

I see the women of my former student's family walking the woods. It's early spring, their breath steams, they are still wearing heavy jackets against the cold. Maybe it's even early enough for the last traces of snow to cling to that fall's moldering leaves. And out of that dream it comes to me: I see a woman standing beside

Wildcat Creek. She's wearing an old barn coat of her husband's and a scarf. She's holding one of the thorns, looking at it, examining it. Then suddenly—in one swift, piercing motion—she jabs the thorn into her palm and pulls it out. Like needle and thread, a long string of blood trails from her hand to the tip of the thorn. Then she does it again. And again. Where is her family? What would make her do something like this? Out of the questions, I piece together a story, a possibility. This woman had two lovely daughters, strong and healthy farm girls. But one of them had been killed. A little more than a year ago. In a car accident.

In the meantime the younger surviving daughter, in her grief, became sullen and morose, the kind of teenager who makes jokes about suicide that aren't funny. They live on a hobby farm, the kind my ex-wife grew up on. A few head of cattle, a flock of sheep. The father teaches fifth grade. The mother is a secretary for the church they go to and is also the church's janitor. She cleans room after room—the Sunday-school rooms, the minister's office, the sanctuary. She is the strong one, the one who has to hold it together for everyone else's sake. The one stabbing her palm.

This is the story of the last time they gather thorns for a crown to put on the altar at church. The end of a family tradition.

Another loss.

The mother and the surviving daughter have been fighting lately, and today—as they walk through the woods—it escalates. To the daughter, going on like nothing has changed is a betrayal of her sister. To the mother, not going on means admitting that her daughter isn't coming back.

With money tight after last year's funeral expenses and a hike in property taxes, it has become impossible for the family to stay on their hobby farm. They can't make the mortgage and will have to sell their cows and sheep. The farm will be sectioned off and sold to developers. The neighbors all around them—retired farmers whose kids went to college and moved out of state—have already sold. It's only a matter of time. And this is what escalates the fight. The daughter loves the farm and these woods and doesn't want to move. As they approach the honey locust and begin picking off thorns, the mother has what she thinks is a bit of good news. Her cousin, a businessman from Chicago, has expressed an interest in buying the farm as a summer getaway.

"A summer getaway?" the daughter says.

"It'll still be in the family."

The daughter isn't having any of it. She didn't want to come on this errand, she doesn't want to sell the farm, and she can't abide in trying to look on the bright side. "They'll slaughter the sheep," she says.

Then she says that maybe they're lucky, the sheep. It is one comment too many for the mother—she has lost one daughter and will not lose another one. Beyond angry, she takes a thorn and stabs her palm. She holds it up to her daughter. "Is this what you want?" she says, holding up her bleeding hand, clenching her teeth. She thrusts that hand before the daughter's face and asks her again, "Is this what you want?" The daughter says nothing. She is shocked. Afraid.

Eventually, the mother pulls her hand away, makes a fist, feeling for the first time the bright, throbbing pain. She is suddenly sorry. She drops to her knees, gasping, sobbing. The daughter takes the scarf from around her neck and carefully begins to wrap her mother's hand.

They kneel in the woods on a cool spring day, no one around for miles. Sunlight whitens the sky.

ONE AFTERNOON, LOST IN THE DREAM of this story, I hear voices. I've been lying on my bed in the back of the house, staring at the ceiling, imagining each scene as though it's projected there and I can watch it like a movie. And I hear voices. The distinct rhythmic murmur of conversation. I slip out onto the deck and look around and for a moment think I'm going crazy because there's no one to be seen. Then they call hello and startle me—a pair of grubby-looking teenage boys sauntering down the driveway.

"We scared him," one of them says.

The other one looks up from the device in his hands, what looks like the joystick to a remote-control airplane. He nods.

They are both sandy haired, thin, strong, sixteen or seventeen at the most, wearing dirty blue jeans and tank tops and scuffed sneakers. "We didn't park you in," says the one who said they scared me. "I know there's a sign up there at the gate says don't park you in, so we didn't. You can get out if you want to."

"It's our hounds," the other says.

"We lost them."

"We didn't lose them."

"Yeah, it's not that we lost them."

"They're down there at the river." The one raises his remote control. "We radio-collared 'em. So we were just wanting to go and get 'em back now. That's why we didn't park you in. We were just wanting to get 'em back."

In Bradley's manual the rules explicitly state that all trespassers are to be asked kindly to return to their point of entry and leave the homestead posthaste. But the manual doesn't say what to do if their goddamn hounds are down at the river and they're "just wanting to get 'em back." I look at the boys and think it over, shrugging to let them know I'm not happy about this. Right next to the sign that says "No Parking" is one that says "No Trespassing"—hadn't they seen that one? And how come they hadn't followed their hounds' route to the river? Something isn't right about this whole thing, but I'm not much interested in getting to the bottom of it. Finally I just shrug again and tell them to hurry up. Go. I point in the direction of the trail to the river. Make it snappy.

When they are gone I get back to work on my story, rereading whole sections of it, wondering if it's too heavy with symbolism—a crown of thorns, a bleeding hand? I've not tried to play these things up, I've tried just to tell it straight, but I still don't know. Every so often as I work along, I look out at the forest, the trail the boys have gone down. An hour passes. Two. I had planned on taking a walk to the river myself today, just to clear my head of all these questions, but now I'm stuck waiting on these boys and their hounds. I pour a glass of water, sit on the deck with a book.

Three hours pass.

Four.

Now I'm getting pissed off. It's late in the afternoon, and there's been no sign of them. I'll have to find them myself.

Filled with a hermit's self-righteous anger at having his wilderness idyll mocked by a couple of teenagers, I throw some water bottles in my backpack, grab my walking stick, and hit the trail. As it happens, they are already on their way back. Our paths cross halfway down to the river. The boys are sweaty and exhausted, their faces streaked with dirt. They've got their radio-collared hounds—big brown dogs, some kind of shepherd mix—leashed and muzzled. Since it's a hot day, upper nineties, and they headed off to the river with only their remote control and the clothes on their backs, I feel obliged to offer them my water. They both readily accept. We stand in the middle of the forest, in the middle of the trail, in the middle of a hot summer afternoon, I with arms crossed, annoyed, and the two of them sweating and panting and drinking my water. They tell me the hounds were three miles upriver to the east, that they'd had to swim across to get them, then swim back with them. The Rogue has a powerful current, and I'm surprised to hear that the boys and their hounds had been able to swim across it.

"It wasn't too bad," one says, taking a long gulp of water, panting, then pouring water on his cap and putting it back on his head. "But it was still cold. You wouldn't think it could be so cold. Not in June."

"Your collars worked," I say.

"They're for hunting."

"Oh, yeah?"

"For tracking bear."

"Or cougar," the other says.

They inform me that cougar hunting in this region has recently been outlawed. The one with the remote control purses his lips and spits a frothy hawker at his feet, rubs it into the soil with the toe of his boot. "It's about time they bring it back," he says. "Before some hiker or somebody gets killed."

By my calculation these boys have walked two miles from the top of the road to the cabin, then another three to find their hounds. Then they swam across a powerful river and back. Then hiked another three miles back to the trail and are now climbing eight hundred vertical feet, with another two miles uphill to go, to get back to their rig. All on no water except what I've given them (unless they chanced giardiasis in one of the creeks) and no food. And it occurs to me that this is how it should be. Today will be a day of legendary proportions for these two, a testament to the idiocy of youth. I imagine them talking about it when they're older—the time they scrabbled through the wilderness after their hounds. It's something I envy them, because I remember days similarly spent.

And maybe because I envy them this day and want some of its magic for myself, I decide to continue on my walk instead of escorting them up the trail, giving them a ride to their rig, and watching them disappear around a bend. Which is exactly what I should do. What I would have done had I been thinking. But instead, hoping to seem to them nonchalant and unafraid, the kind of person they would be foolish to mess with, I say I'll expect them to be gone by the time I get back. I take off to the river. And the whole way down, I wonder if they'll try to break into the cabin.

The idiocy of youth is nothing compared to the idiocy of age and experience. Once to the river, I start back up the trail.

Fortunately, by the time I return the boys are gone. No windows in the cabin have been busted out, the door is still locked, the garden hasn't been bothered. I go check the upper house—it's fine as well. I've been lucky.

A few days later, however, on a walk to the pond, I notice a metallic gleam under the low-hanging bow of a Douglas fir and discover two cans of seltzer water and an empty tin of sardines. I pick up the trash, not thinking much of it, until I return to the cabin and see in the breezeway a six-pack of seltzer water (from John Daniel's winter leftovers) with two cans missing. I just shake my head. The little shits.

IN OTHER NEWS, THE BAIT has done the trick on the mice. No more scrabbling in the breezeway or the wall space behind my headboard. No more roly-poly black turds on the shelves, nests in my dresser drawer. But I don't have poison—the prescription variety—to cure my guilt. Now instead of lying awake listening to the mice, it's my mind that does the scrabbling. The poison in the bait is a chemical called bromadiolone, an anticoagulant that causes hemorrhaging—death from the inside out. I've seen several mice suffering its effects. They don't run when they see me in the breezeway. Rather, they just stumble like drunks, tripping over their own feet. They fall and pick themselves up, fall and pick themselves up. Out of pity I crush their skulls with my boot.

I'll never like using poison. I don't like handling it, and I don't like how it enters the food chain. After the mouse dies, something will eat it. A snake, a bird, a pile of maggots. Its body will break down, and the chemicals will enter the watershed. Maybe one poisoned mouse—or a hundred poisoned mice, a thousand, a

Ownership

hundred thousand—won't be enough to do any significant damage to an ecosystem (i.e., to the extent that it affects humans). But what troubles me isn't so much the science as it is the ethics: chemical warfare for ease and convenience.

And I realize my own culpability here—I don't want to spend the time and energy figuring out how to solve my rodent problems, so instead I nuke them. The irony is that, ostensibly, I have come to this remote homestead to learn about Nature with a capital N. To meditate on wilderness, on wildness. Only instead of apprenticing myself to the most basic concerns of such a life—and keeping rodents out of one's wilderness cabin is surely one of the most basic—I'm cheating myself of any real learning by opting for short-term solutions to long-term problems. It's a poisoning of the mind and the imagination, and what hemorrhages is a sense of responsibility to anything beyond my own comfort. But I do it, time and again. When the bait is gone, I put out another. I step on the poison-drunk mice and crush their skulls and kick their tiny, smashed-up bodies into the weeds. It's as though the mice, pitying me my ignorance, keep offering their lives so that some part of me might understand how much they have to teach if only I would listen.

Up at the pond it's a similar story. Some kind of weedy lily pad has begun to take over, and Bradley has asked that I spray it with Cutrine. The pond's for fire-suppression purposes, to potentially save the houses, and so I do it. One morning, before it gets too hot, I put on gloves and goggles, mix a batch of the chemicals in a sprayer, and head up to the pond. I work my way along the water's edge.

The poison is almost pretty, squirting out in a fine mist, making a rainbow where it catches the light. It hits the water, dissolves. The newts swim on, unaware, uncaring. A green bullfrog watches me knowingly.

It's probably a safe-enough product—I don't really know. But afterward I shed my gloves and goggles and sit in the grass, looking out at the water, vaguely depressed. I remember the day I saw a barred owl in a tree across the meadow. I remember Bradley's kids, Wilder and Hollynd, laughing in the forest. How to square those good feelings with what I feel right now? The innocence of children versus the poison I spread? There is no real answer, only time, perspective. Only the big quiet hovering over everything like mist. Maybe the quiet here is enough. Maybe it has to be.

I watch a dragonfly nymph on the end of a long blade of grass. Sometime in the past few hours it has emerged from the water, climbed to this perch, and begun to shed its shell. I can see its thin blue abdomen, its white wings. They are wet, sticky looking, still too heavy to lift. Dragonflies are the insects I most associate with my father, our fishing trips. The way a pair of them would land on the tip of his rod and flutter off, chasing each other in wild zigzags. But this one, on its wind-bent blade of grass, is a thing so small and vulnerable. Fearing that it might fall in the water and get eaten up, I grab my walking stick and offer it as a safer, more sturdy plank for the dragonfly to crawl out onto. And of course—of course—in my clumsiness, in my thinking I can improve upon hundreds of millions of years of evolution, I accidentally knock it into the water, where it drowns.

"O kind and terrible love, which You have given me," writes Thomas Merton in a long prayer in *Thoughts in Solitude*, "and which could never be in my heart if You did not love me! . . . I am seen by You under the sky, and my offenses have been forgotten by You—but I have not forgotten them.

"Only one thing I ask: that the memory . . . should not make me afraid to receive into my heart the gift of Love."

If anything redeems the hemorrhaging mice, the drowned dragonfly, the knowing bullfrog glancing up at me as chemicals rain down on his head and home, it's that the love I feel here—the

Ownership

kind and terrible love—is large enough, empty enough, to ingest the poison of my transgressions without itself becoming contaminated. Regardless of my fear and ineptitude, my faithlessness, my feelings of being unworthy for the gift that has been set in front of me, moments of grace somehow come.

On a walk to the river I stop in the meadow where I found bear scat and a deer antler my first week here alone. I sit down to rest, surrounded by blue wildflowers. I look at the sky, the clouds, the trees.

Not six inches from my boots—my mouse-skull-crushing boots—a hummingbird appears, pushing its face into the wildflowers all around me, tasting their nectar. It has a ruby stain on its throat, what look like iridescent green scales under its wings, brown and orange bars on its tail feathers. Nuzzling one flower after the next, it is oblivious to me. Its tiny shining body. This mountain meadow.

Another time it is coming on dusk, and I am doing a sink full of dishes that I've let go for too long. I've drawn hot water into the sink basin and am scrubbing away, rinsing, setting plates and glasses and silverware on an old dishtowel on the counter. The work is meditative. I'm thinking of the Buddhist monk Thich Nhat Hahn who said to wash each dish as though you were washing the baby Buddha. With nothing else to do out here but welcome the night ahead, its promise of books and loneliness, the oncoming dark, it's not hard to imagine each dish as somehow holy. It feels good to do something simple with my hands. Something gentle. It feels like a kind of forgiveness.

Then from outside, a movement catches my eye—some kind of low-flying bird, perhaps a wood grouse, streaking down from the hillside on tottering wings and colliding with the garden fence. It's the sound of a fouled-off baseball connecting with a chain-link backstop. I shake my hands dry and hustle out to investigate. I want to know what kind of bird it is, maybe collect a stray feather or two, a story. But down in the garden I don't find anything. No feathers, no bird. Just the apple trees at dusk, the sky a smoky purple, a half-moon rising over Rattlesnake Ridge. And though I've found no evidence of the bird and my sink full of dishes is waiting inside, the water getting cold, something tells me to be still, to wait. I stand in the garden, in the long grass under the apple trees. The forest beyond is dark and ominous. Out of the silence I hear the sound of a large animal rustling in the undergrowth, headed my way. To see a bear at this distance. To be so near. I crouch low, wait, and after a moment he emerges: one of the black-tailed deer, Cougar-Bait's friend, chest deep in the blackberry canes.

Ownership

7

THE OTHER SIDE

OF THE MOUNTAIN

Several miles west of the homestead a backpacking trail rises three hundred feet above the Rogue, offering breathtaking views of the canyon. From this height the river resembles a snakeskin, elastic and alive, great fluid muscles at work just below the surface. The white-water rafters—their rafts ever present now that the spring rains have passed and the temperatures have risen—float like pale scales down the snake's sun-dappled back. One day I watch four bright rafts at a sandbar across the channel. A dozen or so sunburned men and women emerge in khaki shorts, tank tops, and floppy hats, and begin unloading their supplies, setting up camp. They have brought coolers of beer and food, a portable cookstove/barbecue grill assembled on the beach, several big dome tents, waste buckets that they set fifty yards outside camp. Once everything's been unloaded, a woman slips away from the pack and approaches the water's edge, kicks off her flip-flops, pulls her loose white T-shirt over her head, and lets it drop to the sand. She's got on a neon-green bikini top, frayed cut-off jeans. She wades into the water, which even though it's mid-June is still ice-cold, and the swift current throws her off-balance. Her arms flare out. She steadies herself and eases in farther, bends deeply at the waist, splashes water onto her chest and arms. Finally, she takes a deep breath and submerges. The neon-green bikini top radiates under the waves, the only part of her still visible. When she comes up for air she shakes her head and wipes her eyes, blows a bit of water from her lips.

Soon two more women join her, slipping out of their clothes and into the river. From my perch high above them, my back against a canyon wall, half in and half out of shadow, I have to fight the urge to call down and wave hello. Better that they not know I'm here, that they not know there's a cabin nearby.

All that keeps me from being swept away by loneliness is the *chee-reek* of an osprey in the broken crown of a Douglas fir, raising its wings in agitation, spitting vitriol about the commotion down on the beach.

I study the speckled patterns of its gorgeous brown and white wing markings, the dark bands at its eyes.

Chee-reek. Chee-reek.

I'm not as alone as I thought.

One morning a few days later, I'm visited by a mating pair of western tanagers. While sitting at my breakfast table and staring at my laptop, lost in the dream of a story I'm writing, something slams like a fist—*boom! boom!*—into the sliding glass door on the deck. The first thing I think is that those boys with their radio-collared hounds have come back to get me. Outside, however, there's nothing. Just my truck in the drive, the apple trees, the garden. Then I see them: the male with his bright-red head, the female with her yellow wing bars. They lie lifeless on the deck. Their wings are outstretched, limp, and their tiny beaks gape open. I quickly put together the story of what's happened. So relentless and all-consuming was their pursuit of one another that they came crashing into the glass at full speed. One moment at the height of life, the next dead. I pick them up, hold one in each hand. They are light, delicate, *intricate*. Later I'll attempt a poem and call them my teachers, halves of an incomplete heart, but right now they are not ideas or metaphors, they are just dead birds—pretty little things—limp in my hands. I take them to the garden, lay them in a bed of grass under the apple trees.

Later I decide I should commemorate their lives with a photograph. So I grab my camera, slip back to the garden. Only when I get there, the birds are gone. I'd seen a garter snake in the grapevines yesterday—could the snake have devoured them? Or were they not really dead but only stunned, unconscious?

There is no way to know for sure. The cynical part of me—the realist—thinks snake, thinks dead and devoured.

But since there is no way to know, I can't rule out the possibility that first one and then the other began to stir and come to, rekindled by the slow summer breeze; that one and then the other carefully stood up and shook out its wings and snorted back to life; that after this respite, their courtship continued.

BRADLEY RINGS ME UP ON THE satellite phone to let me know that Frank's son, Ian, and his new bride, Jenny Oakes, are set for a midsummer arrival next week, a honeymoon, and will stay for several days at the upper house. Bradley lets me know that I am not to bother them. He has to say this because it's one of those things a person has to say. But does he really think I'd be a third wheel on their honeymoon? I'm still licking my wounds from a divorce, after all, and it's not as though images of marital bliss will make me feel better. To say nothing of the reminder honeymooners will be about my own romantic prospects out here. Am I supposed to get dressed up and head to town like some kind of throwback to the gold-mining days? Should I take out an ad online: divorced white male seeks female companion for experiment in backcountry solitude? It's bad enough that on orientation weekend Joe Green mentioned that a cute woman worked at the Rand Ranger Station last summer. Every time I drive by now I think about looking her up. In my imagination, we hit it off and fall in love, and pain falls away from me forever.

In the meantime, figuring that the honeymooners will want to spend their days at the river, I start tearing down the corral fence—a project that will keep me busy and out of their hair. I put on a thick flannel shirt, leather gloves. The rotting quarter-split rails come out easily enough, and I drag them to a big pile in front of the barn, where next spring when it's wet Bradley can burn them. The posts are another story. Buried two feet deep in Oregon clay, I dig all around them with a spade, rock them back and forth, push on them with my full weight. I karate kick them, beg and plead, curse, cajole. The first one takes me half an hour. I carry it to the burn pile, dump it off, and start back for the next one. The corral fence stretches out of sight behind the barn.

On the day of Ian and Jenny's arrival, I hear their truck at the upper house and tell myself they're not even here, that for all intents and purposes I'm alone. The feeling isn't altogether different, I imagine, from how the deer who got zapped by the garden fence feels as he nonchalantly circles the apple trees inside.

When I finally see the honeymooners bumping down the drive in their truck, I take a deep breath and wave a gloved hand as though I'm not a crazy person. They see it in my eyes. "You look about how Jenny looked," Ian says after we've made our initial introductions. "You think?" he says to Jenny.

"A little touched," Jenny says.

They are a good-looking couple—tan, strong, laid-back,

outdoorsy. Late twenties, early thirties. They live in Walla Walla, Washington, where Ian is a printmaker and the director of a university art museum and Jenny is a poet and teacher. They met while Jenny was the writer-resident in 1999. Ian had come for a visit, they'd hit it off, and the rest was history. Now they're on their honeymoon and have arrived with gifts for the homestead. Ian opens the back of their rig and begins pulling out plant after plant: a butterfly bush, an apricot tree, a bald cypress. "They're going to need plenty of water this summer," Ian says to me, nodding. "For the roots to really get established."

"I'll keep them watered," I say.

The following afternoon I'm out working on the fence again, kicking the posts and wedging them out of the clay, dragging them to the burn pile, when Ian and Jenny roll up, ready to get their hands dirty in the garden.

From the barn they take out a wheelbarrow and a shovel, a garden rake, a pair of loppers, a posthole digger. I make an effort to look busy and aloof, but I keep an eye on their progress. One of the things they do is a good pruning of the apple trees. Ian mans the loppers, and Jenny piles the switches outside the garden fence. When they're through pruning, they start pitching fallen apples into the forest.

That evening, after I've taken a shower and put on clean clothes, I head up to the upper house, where I have been invited for dinner. Ian cooks brats on the grill, and Jenny whips up her version of Bradley's guacamole. We eat on the deck—paper plates, cans of Tecate—and the sun goes down, turning the sky over the mountains an ashen gray. Ian tells a story about an overly amorous dog of Jenny's that tried to assault a duck in a public park. Jenny tells one about seeing a cougar with kittens skitter up the driveway. And one about seeing an elk. "Its rack was about as wide," she says, spreading her arms apart, "as the grille of your truck." I tell them that on my first day here last summer we saw a bald eagle and a bear, a couple of snakes. I do my impersonation of Bradley banging his grill tongs and calling the bear names. It's all good fun, and I feel lucky to have been invited up here tonight. Not only are Ian and Jenny the picture of newlywed bliss, but they are also smart and funny and filled with good stories.

"I planted that bald cypress for my grandfather," Ian says when talk turns to the garden and the planting that he and Jenny have done. "It can live to be forty-five hundred years old. It's a very famous tree over in Japan."

"Ian studied in Asia," Jenny says.

"One of my favorite writers is from Japan," I say. "Yasunari Kawabata. *Thousand Cranes. Beauty and Sadness.*"

The talk goes on like that, each story a tributary of the next. Then finally it's dark and I'm half drunk and know it's time to go, but I don't really want to go. An evening of meeting new friends and talking after these weeks and months alone feels like a gift to savor. But it's their honeymoon, and I've promised Bradley to not get in the way. So finally I thank them again for the meal, bid them goodnight, and, no longer needing a flashlight or lantern to light my way, I walk home in the dark.

AT THE END OF THE WEEK, the day Ian and Jenny are set to leave, they show me the bald cypress in honor of Ian's grandfather. Halfway between the lower and upper houses, beneath a culvert off the driveway, where springwater seeps out of the hillside in shining rivulets, Ian has fashioned a makeshift reservoir. There in the mud is the sapling. To keep it watered, all I have to do is push a handful of the mud aside and let the water soak in around it. An ingeniously simple design, I'll probably only need to come down here later in the summer, when it dries up. We stand around a few moments, looking down on the garden and the apple trees, and I thank the two of them for the pruning work they've done. You have to go in after the vertical runners, really take them out, Ian explains. You want to encourage horizontal growth. "I mean, think about it," he says. "You don't want to have to climb so high to get at your apples."

"It's how Graiff died," Jenny says.

Graiff is Bill Graiff, one of the homestead's original inhabitants. The foundation of his little cabin lies crumbling and ruined not far from where we stand. "He fell out of a tree, didn't he? Fell out," Jenny says to Ian, who nods, "and broke his hip. Managed to crawl back to his cabin."

I look down at the garden, at the three or four big apple trees—trees that Graiff and Dutch Henry, the homestead's namesake, had planted. "How'd they keep the bears out of the apples without a fence?"

"Well," Jenny says, following my gaze, thinking about it, "I'm guessing they shot everything that moved."

Past the garden is Dutch Henry's barn, the pile of split-rail fence I've taken down and stacked for Bradley to burn next spring. I don't imagine the work of taking it apart was nearly as difficult as the work of chopping the wood, notching the posts, and digging the holes, but it gives me a sense of satisfaction. Where before there had been a fence to corral horses and hold back the meadow, there is now an open field of long grass, wild daisies, and bull thistle. Something's been set free.

Ian and Jenny and I chat a while longer about Dutch Henry and Graiff and the homestead's legacy in the river canyon. Like Frank, Bradley, and Joe Green the weekend of my orientation, Ian and Jenny wish they didn't have to leave. At dinner the other night they'd talked about what it might take for the two of them to come here for an extended stay, a year or more—the money they'd need, how to take the time off from work. I could imagine them making it happen, living the dream, and it's something that even though I am here right now, living my own dream, I already envy them. Before I got here last April, I never once thought of the wilderness as a place to call home, or as a place in which to love and be loved. And now? Now I do.

THE FIRST FEW DAYS AFTER Ian and Jenny leave are good ones. In the garden my peas are ripe and delicious. The sweet corn has gotten tall and sprouted tassels. I can pull a stalk to me to breathe the pollen scent of home. I start to realize that everything I'm learning out here—about myself, about the natural world—could have been learned back home, but only coming here could have taught me that. And because I'm feeling good, because I keep learning what seem like big lessons, I happily get to work digging up bull thistles and mowing one last time in the garden. When I'm not out working, I'm reading and writing. On a bulletin board John Daniel had tacked up some lines by Ezra Pound that somehow say it all:

> *And the days are not full enough*
> *And the nights are not full enough*
> *And life slips by like a field mouse*
> *Not shaking the grass.*

As at home in my life as I am these days, however, it is only a matter of time before feelings as familiar as my face return: loneliness, sadness. My failed marriage is a razor blade I use to scrape them smooth.

My failure *at* marriage.

In my mind, there is an image, a moment, just as poisonous and potent as the Just One Bite I feed to the mice in the breezeway. On the night I tell my wife I think we have made a mistake getting married—news that comes at her out of the blue—we lie awake in bed. She is sobbing deeply. Like I have never heard anyone sob, not even at a funeral. Lying beside her, I want to disappear. I want to die. In my mind I plead with her: stop crying, stop crying, *stop crying*. But since I can't ask her to do that, I just lie down beside her and listen to her awful sobbing.

Four years later, the merest thought of that night, and I am back there as though I have never left. And maybe I haven't. That's another fantasy of mine—that I have split in two, that one part of me stayed with her, is with her still, in some dream I can't imagine. The other part is here in the wilderness.

Maybe my life has forked apart like a river and will someday, on the other side of the mountain, rejoin itself.

Maybe not.

Last winter, to begin to deal with some of these feelings and to prepare myself for solitude, I joined a meditation group. A friend had invited me. We met once a week in the basement of St. Tom's, a Catholic church on Purdue's campus, and watched instructional videos about Centering Prayer, discussed the week's practice, and sat together in silence for twenty minutes. Centering Prayer is as simple as it is peaceful. You choose a sacred word (I chose *stone*), and whenever you notice yourself slipping into a thought—whether it's daydreaming, planning, or plotting revenge—you gently remind yourself of your word and let it serve as a symbol of your intention to be present in this individual moment with God. The point is not to keep yourself from thinking but to enlarge your capacity to stay in the here and now.

I remember one of the group's participants, a man named Phil who worked for the church in some administrative capacity, perhaps fund-raising. He was a short Italian with a pepper-and-salt goatee, always in a suit and tie. On my first night of meditating we'd begun our twenty minutes of silence when some teenagers came downstairs and, not realizing that we were in the other room with the door closed, had started laughing and horsing around. I heard Phil's chair scrape across the concrete floor, the door open, and then a hushed shout, "Shhhh! We're trying to meditate!"

It made me laugh. I liked Phil.

The one time I talked to him, a few weeks later, I mentioned my trepidation about coming to Oregon to be alone. I mentioned my ex-wife and how I hadn't gotten over some of the things that had happened. It was a cold night, February maybe, and I guess I thought he might offer me some kind of wisdom.

He nodded for a second, then blew a warm breath into his hands and rubbed them together. He looked me in the eye. "It sounds like . . ." he said. "It sounds like, well, maybe it's time to let go of some of that."

He was right—of course, he was right. But I walked away from the conversation disappointed because I didn't have a clue about *how* to let go. I still don't. Maybe it's a matter of wanting to badly enough. Maybe if you want to badly enough you'll learn how. Which is how I learned to write. Hours and hours of staring into a computer screen, struggling to craft a clean sentence, tinkering with length and word choice and tone, then reading it over later and deleting it all. It's how I survived those first rocky months after the divorce. I rented a grungy efficiency on South Fourth Street and gave myself over to the discipline of writing: every day for two hours at a sit. It gave me something to do, something outside myself to focus on. But by that winter, by the time I had learned I'd be coming to Oregon, I knew it was time to start working on myself.

I come across an opportunity in a book my friend Patricia (the one who got me started with the meditation group at St. Tom's) has sent me. The book is *A Path with Heart: A Guide through the Perils and Promises of Spiritual Life* by Jack Kornfield, a clinical psychologist who trained as a Buddhist monk in Thailand before returning to the West, where he now teaches Insight Meditation.

The opportunity is a meditation.

Roughly translated, you are to close your eyes and meditate upon a particularly painful moment in your life. At the height of your pain, you are to imagine a knock on the door. You go to answer, and it is Jesus. Or Buddha. Or Mother Mary. Some wise figure in whom you can trust. You walk your chosen person over to the painful scene from your past and watch as, for a moment, that person takes over your body and does with it what he or she would do in this situation. Once what is done is done, your person leans in and whispers a bit of wisdom in your ear and quickly goes away.

One night, after I've eaten dinner and washed the dishes, dried them, put them away—anything to put it off—I sit down in the rocking chair on the deck to do this meditation. I get comfortable, relax, take a last look out at Rattlesnake Ridge, and close my eyes. I am lying in bed beside my wife, who is curled up, sobbing. Unable to stop. She has her back to me, and I see her straight blonde hair, the back of her neck, her ear. Every part of her is convulsing. In my mind I plead: stop crying, stop crying, *stop crying*. Then there is a knock at the door, and it is Jesus. He is wearing a flowing white robe. His beard is sparse. I lead him over to the bed, and he looks down at my sobbing wife. He nods and lies down beside her, and for a moment the two of us—Jesus and I—are one person. He puts his arms around her, holds her. I put my arms around her, hold her. He says nothing; I say nothing. He lets her pain and sadness flow into him; I let her pain and sadness flow into me. I sit with that pain. I don't run from it or judge it or try to wish it away. It is simply here, raw and exposed, just as I am simply here.

After a few moments, Jesus rises from the bed, and I show him back to the door. Before he leaves, he leans down and whispers into my ear: "Her life is more than this moment. This isn't the end of anything."

Then he is gone.

I open my eyes, blink. The sun has all but disappeared in the west, and Rattlesnake Ridge is a simmering brick red.

Then slowly, slowly, as the sun slips away, the ridge fades from red to chocolate brown. From brown to dark blue. From dark blue to black. I feel it out there, hovering in the darkness. I hear the river plunging over boulders, frothing up in big eddies. *Her life is more than this moment. This isn't the end of anything.*

A FEW DAYS LATER, after my morning writing, I slip down to the garden to water Ian and Jenny's new plantings. As I'm giving everything a good drink—the apricot tree, the big butterfly bush—I look at their pile of apple switches outside the fence, look at the pile of fence rails and posts I've stacked before the barn. It's the physical manifestation of our time here. Our work. And thinking of that, I remember something from my visit last summer over the Fourth of July weekend. There had been a rickety old bench—part of an ancient picnic table—up at the pond. By the time my father and I arrived this spring, however, it had finally succumbed to the winter wet and collapsed. One day while we mowed, I gathered up the pieces and tossed them into the woods.

I haven't given that bench a second thought until now, standing in the garden in full morning sun, watering the fruit trees. Until looking at the pile of switches and the old rotted fence it took me a week to disassemble.

I should make a new one.

A new bench.

Taken with the idea, I turn off the hose and head for the barn. On its far side is a pile of skinny barkless logs left over from the construction of the cabin's deck railing. I pick three sturdy pieces, about eight feet long, the thickness of my calves, for the main bench. I grab two more, the thickness of my ankles, for backing and support. I lug it all to my truck and toss it in the back. Next I grab two big madrone rounds from beside the woodshed, roll them to my rig, and heft them up and in.

I drive to the upper house, where I find a tray of big nails in the shed, and a claw hammer, a roll of twine. I have a base in the rounds, something to sit on in the rails, nails to keep it all together, and twine for decoration. I think that's all I need. The only thing I've ever built before—and I didn't build it so much as help my father by holding the tools—was a rabbit trap when I was a kid. This is something different. I zip up to the pond and unload the rounds, roll them to where I want them. I drop the rails nearby, load the nails in my pockets, get to work hammering and figuring, standing back to make sure it'll all come together. In an hour or so, I've fashioned a beautifully rustic bench. I wrap twine around the three bottom rails. It will rot away by next spring, but I like how it marries the rails' smoothness and the roughness of the rounds. I sit on the bench and look at the newts in the pond, look out over the meadow I've cleared of ferns and Douglas fir saplings. The bench is creaky and uncomfortable. Knots in the wooden rails knuckle into my back. There are some big purple-black carpenter ants that live in the rounds and aren't thrilled about this arrangement. All in all, it's not a place you'd want to sit for very long. But it's mine. Mine. I'll sit here all day if I feel like it.

8

HEAT OF THE

SUMMER

THERE IS NOTHING MORE MEDITATIVE THAN dry hundred-degree heat. Up at the pond I take off my clothes, lay them out on the bench I made, and swim naked with the newts. On the trail to the river, where a tiny icy creek comes charging out of the mountain-side, I sit on a stone and let the water splash over me. Nothing keeps the heat off for good, and after a few of these vain attempts at refreshment—the effects of which are so brief as to be of negligible value—I give up. Better just to endure the warmth, to work around its edges: late at night, early in the morning. A day that peaks at a hundred and two degrees at four in the afternoon will drop to seventy by midnight, sixty by dawn.

In the heat, there's a stillness to the world. The birds, the deer, the fence lizards on the deck—everything seems lethargic, everything waits. Time passes like the big brown wasps gently buzzing the deck rails.

Most days, I am content to wait out the heat in the shade of the big Douglas fir by the barn. I fill a jug with water, grab a blanket and a book, and read until I fall asleep. Though I am a fiction writer first and foremost, the work that speaks to me most directly out here has been poetry. Especially the poems of Walt Whitman, whose long lines wrap around me like the twisty tendrils of a grapevine.

> *I do not doubt that the orbs and the systems of the orbs play*
> *their swift sports through the air on purpose and that I shall*
> *one day be eligible to do as much as they, and more than they,*
> *I do not doubt that temporary affairs keep on millions and*
> *millions of years.*   FROM "ASSURANCES"

Back home in Indiana this is the time of stifling humidity, raging thunderstorms. Every third or fourth day dark clouds pile up on the horizon, followed in short order by a pounding rain. Here it's dry and hasn't rained since May. The muddy driveway that this spring threatened to swallow my truck and its street treads is now hard as baked clay. Walking down it my feet kick up a fine, powdery dust. To keep the garden green I have to let the sprinkler run all night long. It is one of the fine sounds of summer, its slow *tick-tick-tick* barely audible behind the chorus of crickets and locusts. In the mornings I turn it off and take a garden hose to the corners of the garden the sprinkler doesn't reach. I stand in the sunlight among the wet, dripping trees. If over the night any apples have fallen, I toss them under the snag of a dead Douglas fir below the garden. Where Ian and Jenny tossed them. Where the deer have learned to find a snack.

Lately I have been trying to hand-feed apples to the deer. One of the big bucks will come within ten feet of me, staring warily

Heat of the Summer

into my eyes, hungrily at the apple in my outstretched hand. But he'll come no closer. I'm afraid of getting gored by his antlers, or pummeled by his hooves, and it might just be that my fear extends around me in a protective ten-foot arc. I don't know. Eventually, I toss him the apple, watch the juice froth his black lips. And sometimes when I see the three of them, I'll throw two apples far away and watch the big bucks go chasing after them. When they're gone, I'll gently lob one over to Cougar-Bait.

Cougar-Bait looks at the apple and looks at me. Then he looks at the other two, to see if he can get away with this. They're out in the meadow, searching for the apples I tossed. Cougar-Bait lowers his head and, using his front teeth, rips off a swatch of the apple's flesh, quickly chews it, looks around.

Gets away with it.

But the deer are not the only ones who enjoy the apples I toss out of the garden. One night I awaken from a deep sleep to what sounds like someone trying to break into the cabin with an ax. I lie paralyzed with fear, listening. *Thwack! Thwack!* Then a moment or two of silence, and it comes again. *Thwack!* It's not coming from inside the cabin. It's farther off. I get out of bed and grab a headlamp flashlight. Out on the deck it is a cool, quiet, and dark night. So quiet I start to wonder if I haven't dreamed the whole thing.

Then I hear another thwack out in the woods, followed by the heavy, brushy foot-dragging I have come to associate with the homestead's bears. I put on my headlamp and raise a pair of binoculars.

It's hard at first to adjust the focus of the binoculars to the headlamp's meager projection power, but soon enough I strike a balance: I see the garden fence, grapevines, apple trees—all dimly lit. Nothing. No bear. Then it hits me: the apples I threw out under the snag. I glass the dead Douglas fir and am met with a pair of fiery, shining eyes. The bear is looking up at me, startled by my headlamp. Whether it's angry or afraid or merely curious, I can't tell. All I see are the eyes, glowing like embers. The bear's body, black against the black sky, the black trees, is a vague silhouette. When it turns its head, the eyes disappear, and I lose all sight of it. If not for the continued *thwack-thwack* I wouldn't know it was even there. But why is the bear attacking the dead tree? It hits me again: the apples I threw out. The bear thinks the dead fir is an apple tree. It's eaten all I tossed there and is thrashing the trunk to make more fall.

I watch the bear until it tires and gives up and moves on, and, satisfied that the action is over for the night, I crawl back into bed. The next morning, after turning off the sprinkler and watering the corners of the garden, I walk back to the snag to investigate. There are torn-up swatches of grass under the Doug fir. Big shredded skeins of bark hang from its trunk where the bear thrashed it. The thought of such power. I look around, wondering if the bear is still nearby, hungry and feeling territorial about what it perceives as its apple tree. I'm not afraid of bears anymore, not like in the beginning. Now I'm just curious, fascinated. I want to know what this bear's life is like out here, how it navigates its days, what it senses and perceives, what it *knows*. It's eaten all the windfall apples I've tossed out. They're gone. Some of them I'd taken big bites out of before pitching them over the fence: does the bear know my scent? If it's this close to the homestead it must. If some of my saliva was still on the apples I bit into, does that mean that a trace of my DNA has nourished the bear? Am I part of the bear's awareness, part of its ancient furry mind, the wildness of his heart?

My only regret is that in solitude I can't share this feeling with anyone. I try to describe my experiences in letters I send to friends. I tell stories to my folks on my weekly trip to town. But nothing captures the way it really feels, and I can't make anyone else understand who doesn't already understand. How

Heat of the Summer

many people know what it's like to spend a week alone? How many people know what a day alone is like? I've been at the homestead some three and a half months now, and while I've had plenty of visitors—Bradley and his kids, Dave Reed from the BLM, the honeymooners—most days it's just me and the deer. Me and the river. Me and the big blue sky.

Every day something beautiful and small. The way the deer can reach their heads around and bite at ticks on their flanks. The way they snort. The way they scratch their ears with their long back legs.

The way bats circle the cabin at dusk, snagging moths and mosquitoes attracted by my propane lamps.

The way tiny slugs glisten on the windfall apples. The way the grooves of a ponderosa pine smell like cream soda. The way rosemary, picked in big clumps from the bush in the garden and crushed between my fingers, evokes eternity. In my journal I write: "If I am dead and you are reading this, pick a sprig of rosemary, crush it, stand alone under a rising moon. I'm not gone."

And today, standing where the bear stood, I understand with deep clarity—for his questions have become my questions—the final passage of "Ktaadn," Thoreau's famous essay: "I stand in awe of my body, this matter to which I am bound has become strange to me. . . . Think of our life in nature,—daily to be shown matter, to come into contact with it,—rocks, trees, wind on our cheeks! the *solid* earth! the *actual world!* the *common sense! Contact! Contact! Who* are we? *where* are we?"

This is the Thoreau I admire most of all. Not the hero living by his own means at Walden Pond; not the pithy craftsman of quotable quotes; not the meticulous, miraculous journal keeper whose observations cut to the quick with the precision of a scientific instrument. No, the Thoreau I admire most is the one struck dumb on a mountaintop in Maine. Struck dumb by the smallness of our accumulated knowledge in the face of raw, depthless reality.

The desolation of Mount Katahdin turns such formerly simple questions as "Who are we, where are we?" into maddening and unanswerable koans to which the only appropriate response is one's whole life, one's being, nothing less. And this is the gift of Thoreau, as I understand it. By virtue of word and deed, this pencil maker's son uses his pencil to free the rest of us from a worldview prescribed by people and institutions who hold fast to power, prestige, and tradition, and who would claim these stations as evidence of a certain knowledge of the truth. But in the *actual* world, on the *solid* earth, what truth is there, and who would be so bold as to name it? Who are we, where are we? To take nothing for granted, not even this—out of deep humility comes the birth of wisdom. The necessity of silence and solitude.

For me, it's a few days after seeing the bear sign that wisdom comes. Maybe it's all the Whitman I've been reading, or maybe it's my meditation practice starting to pay dividends. Late one afternoon, returning from a walk to the pond where the newts are playing it cool, lounging, I round the corner by the upper house and look up the river canyon at a stunning sight: a huge cloud has settled on Rattlesnake Ridge, and the setting sun has turned the cloud a brilliant salmon pink.

The cloud is so big and cleaves so closely to the mountain that everything around me—the long grass in the meadow, the red-dirt driveway, my own skin—also turns pink, glows. I look at my arms, at my hands.

I am an ember.

But as much as this sudden becoming thrills me, it is followed a moment later by melancholy, because I have no one to share it with. And I start to wonder: How many visions just as mighty and as beautiful have I already seen and forgotten since coming here? How many epiphanies will no one else ever know, or that even I might not remember? Then something strange. I hear a voice inside my mind, but it's not my voice. It's the voice of the

Heat of the Summer

grasses in the meadow, or the big cloud itself out on Rattlesnake Ridge, and it says: *The point isn't to remember. The point is to live a life as beautiful as what you see. Then you share it with everyone.*

HAVING SPENT THE BETTER PART of the day reading, writing, thinking, and walking in perfect silence, I am now sitting on the deck. It has been cooler than usual for mid-July, slightly overcast and dreary. This afternoon I watched an intense squabble between Cougar-Bait and his friends and three other deer, all six of them grunting and snorting and rising up on their hind legs to pummel each other. It was like a bar brawl from an old western, and I could imagine Cougar-Bait, in a moment of comedic interlude, bashing one of the invaders over the head with a whiskey bottle. They fought from one end of the driveway to the other, then off into the woods.

I've come out to the deck this evening partly because I'm curious to find out if my friends were victorious in their battle and partly because I've noticed what look like storm clouds forming over the river canyon.

It's been so long since we've had any rain. How I'd love to hear a big full-throated thunderstorm come charging down the mountains, raindrops peppering the dusty red driveway. How good it would feel to fall asleep to a slow drizzle as the storm trails away. But as I think this, I realize that it's an Indiana storm I'm dreaming of, not a southern Oregon storm.

In Indiana a storm's swirling air mass picks up particles of dust that attract condensation, and there is much humidity to aid the process. Here there is little humidity. These clouds are static, dry. When I hear thunder it doesn't boom and clatter so much as it rips like two enormous swatches of Velcro being pulled apart. It sounds sickly, weak. "That all you got?" I laugh at the clouds. Paying me no attention, they keep drifting east. Soon I see the first flashes of lightning, puffs of brightness in the far-off sky. Then as the storm nears I start to make out individual bolts. They shoot across the cloud bottoms in jagged horizontal streaks. They strike at big trees on the ridges in the distance. I start to realize, slowly, stupidly, that it's not going to rain at all. This is an electrical storm. A lightning storm. It hasn't rained for more than a month, and last winter's snows were some kind of record low—it's the middle of a ten-year drought. This place is a tinderbox. I stand up and grip my hands on the deck railing and watch the storm come raging down the canyon, shooting out lightning bolts like an angry god. If a fire started, would I be able to get in my truck and drive to safety? Or would the safest thing be, as fires tend to climb uphill, to hustle down to the river and wait it out? I hope I don't have to decide.

Nothing left to do but let the storm pass, I crawl into bed and lie watching the lightning flicker in the skylight. And I wonder about my friends Cougar-Bait and the others, whether they've won their battle. What do they do when a storm like this blows through? Do they hunker down somewhere, or do they stay on the move, worrying their narrow paths through the forest? Their lives, once they leave the homestead, once they are out of my sight, are a mystery to me. I can piece together some of the story from observation: they meander the forest, browsing grass and other plants; they keep a loose hierarchy, at the bottom of which is the runt Cougar-Bait; they are always on the lookout for danger—twitching their tan, mulish ears at the slightest sound, lifting their noses to sniff the air; if danger is sensed, they bound off stiff-legged. But I can't know what it would be like to wander the forest on a night like tonight, the wind blowing in the trees, lightning shooting across the sky.

Or could I? I think of another of my writer-heroes, John Muir, climbing to the top of a Douglas fir in California to ride out an afternoon thunderstorm. He wanted to know how it felt to be a tree in those gusting High Sierra winds.

Heat of the Summer

Sometimes I wish I had Muir's courage, or Thoreau's passion, or Whitman's huge-heartedness and vision. I think my life could be better, bigger, could mean more to more people. Tonight I am alone and vaguely afraid. Maybe for me courage means admitting that my life's nothing more than what it is.

Maybe courage is admitting that, in the end, my life may be no more knowable to me than the lives of the deer.

The next morning, I wake to sunshine, a day like any other save the yellow-blue haze drifting over the river canyon. Smoke. I get on the satellite phone and call the State Forestry Fire Dispatch Center in Grants Pass, give them my location, ask if I'm in any danger. The man on the other end tells me to hold on, and I hear papers shuffling, clacking keys on a keyboard. When the man comes back he tells me I'm in no danger. There are several fires surrounding the homestead—nine of them, to be precise—but they are all small and don't appear to be too aggressive. I should be sure to call back, he says, if I see anything. I thank him and promise to do so.

Nine fires.

I am ringed by fire.

Later that afternoon, I stand on the deck watching a helicopter work its way up and down the canyon. A long hose hangs from its underside like a limp noodle. Somehow the pilot must hover over a pond somewhere, like the pond farther up the road, and suck water into the hose. Then when he gets over the fire, he lets loose. I never see this part happen—the fires are elsewhere, out of sight—but I can imagine it. What a thrilling and dangerous job. But I can't help but wonder, watching the helicopter buzz down the canyon: what's the wisdom of fire suppression?

On my trip to the homestead last summer, John Daniel had pointed out how the trunks of all the old-growth trees—every last one of them—were black at the bottom, charred. Creeper fires, John explained. They meandered through the forest, crackling and popping, fed by the undergrowth. The bigger trees could endure them. The fire would lap against their trunks like a wave on the shore, but it never reached their crowns. And that's the real danger, a fire spreading crown to crown. But now that we put out the creeper fires—because this timber has a dollar value attached to it, because there is so little forest left that all of it has to be protected, that, in essence, there isn't enough just to let the fire burn itself out—have we made the huge all-encompassing, all-consuming forest fire a permanent fixture of the West? Surely, one thing is clear. In the West fire has become an issue every bit as complicated and contentious as the issue of water.

THOREAU TRAVELED MUCH IN CONCORD, and I travel much from here at the homestead. In my journal I make a long list of the books, stories, essays, and poems that I have read since arriving in April. Some reflect an interest in understanding my solitude more fully. Others offer a much needed escape from solitude. I travel to 1930s Japan with Yasunari Kawabata. E. M. Forster takes me to turn-of-the-century India. I ride the Tubes in London with William Trevor. For companionship I have Thoreau, Whitman, Rainer Maria Rilke, who admonishes me to trust in what is difficult, for what is difficult will never abandon me. And when I close whatever book is in my lap and look out at Rattle-snake Ridge, at the tree with the hole in it—when the quiet of this place again floods over me, floods into me—I feel an almost indescribable surge of gratitude.

I think of what the big pink cloud told me: that the point is not to remember any of this but to live it, to become the gift that has been given to me. Or not to become it—to *be* it. When I am a fiery pink cloud stretching across the sky, there is no more disconnect between myself and my mind and the rest of the world. When I drift over my days filled with light, Thoreau's maddening koan—*Who* are we, *where* are we?—is but a gentle breeze pushing me over the mountains.

The trouble with such epiphanies: they don't last. For days I walk around in a state of bliss and harmony and understanding, hovering from one moment to the next like a hummingbird in a field of blossoms. Everything is gift. Everything sweet. Even my fear of bears, fires, illness, and death—it's all just one big flower to nuzzle for its nectar. Then something pulls me out. The thought of whether I've got enough cash in the bank. The thought of my friend Michelle, seven or eight months pregnant and driving around in an '81 Mercury Cougar without an exhaust pipe. The realization that one of the unintended consequences of designating places like the Rogue River as "Wild and Scenic" is that it gives us license to continue abusing the places we call home, places we have designated "Tame and Ugly"—suburbs sprawling into the countryside, bombed-out inner cities, industrial factories dumping sewage by the ton into the watershed. It pulls me out of my bliss and perhaps rightly so. On the other side of Rattlesnake Ridge is a world of people and problems, incredible injustice, pain. I can't pretend that the stench of suffering doesn't permeate the air even this far outside of town. I can't pretend that I have any answer or antidote. All I have is the quiet of my days, the gift of which sometimes feels like a terrible burden. What will make me worthy?

At the end of the month, hoping to get away from the question for a while (and from my solitary confinement at the homestead), I sign up to go to a writers' conference being held at Southern Oregon University in Ashland. I've heard about it on the local NPR affiliate and been sucked in by an interview with one of the instructors who talked about the significance of place in fiction. It made me start thinking about how much I'd love an afternoon or two with some of my fellow writers. What a nice distraction it would be to talk to someone face-to-face about my writing, maybe even make a friend or a contact for the future. That's what's in my mind, at least, as I set out from the homestead one morning at the end of July: some conviviality and friendship. All the way out to Grants Pass, on the logging roads, on the paved roads, on the highway, I'm tingling with possibility.

Registration for the conference is not until three o'clock that afternoon, so I get to Grants Pass early and make some phone calls, touch base with my parents, chat with Michelle, talk over travel plans with my buddy Big Aaron, who is slated to come visit in two or three weeks. Then I do my laundry and slip through the drive-through at McDonald's, where the same young fifteen-year-old Latina is working. She wants to know if I want a cookie with my lunch. I don't, but I buy one anyway, because she has always been so friendly and nice to me.

Then I go for an oil change—to a place I went to back in May when my serpentine belt crapped out—and realize how lonely I've been. The man changing my oil says, "Thanks for coming back to us."

"You remember me?" I'm flabbergasted. I came to this Oil Can Henry's one time, several months ago, and this man remembers.

"Pardon?"

"You remember me?" I say again.

He furrows his brow slightly and runs the tip of his tongue over his bottom lip, confused. Then he reaches inside my truck and pulls the little sticker off the corner of my windshield—the reminder of when I am due for my next oil change. "The sticker," he says, holding it up. "I seen our sticker up there."

Ashland lies forty miles southeast of Grants Pass, and even though I've talked on the phone and had an oil change, I still arrive two hours early for registration. So I park my truck and walk around downtown. It's a cozy place—shops, outdoor cafés, burbling penny fountains. Berkeley North is how I've heard people describe it. Liberal, moneyed. In the winter, it's a big ski-resort town. In the summer, they host the famous Oregon Shakespeare Festival. After four months at the homestead, more or less alone, walking around like this—like a normal person, like a citizen—feels strange to me. No one here knows who I am. No one knows where I've been, what I've been doing, how I've been living. It's as though I possess a wonderful secret and share it only with my smile. I go to a bookstore, peruse a few titles, buy a Wendell Berry book and a CD of William Stafford's last reading. I have a coffee at a café, thumb through Berry's essays. Then I head back to my truck and the little public park where I've left it. All the concrete in town, the hardness of the sidewalk—it feels so unnatural. In the park, I lie down in the short yellow grass and take a nap.

Later in the afternoon I drive to the university, register for the conference, and am given a parking sticker, a key to a dorm room. There is a "Welcome Breakfast" tomorrow morning at nine, but until then I'm free to do whatever I choose. I could find a restaurant downtown, maybe scalp a ticket to one of the plays, hear some live music at a bar. But instead I spend the evening at the end of the hallway, talking to friends back home on the pay phone. Michelle, Big Aaron, my brother, my mom and dad—the same people I'd already called once today. It's the best thing in the world just to relax and talk with the people who love you. How have I ever taken this for granted?

That night, after grabbing a sub from a sub shop across the street from campus, I take advantage of the dorm's free electricity and open my laptop, work on a new story. When I'm finished it is late, and I'm ready to go to bed. But it's hot, hardly any breeze blowing through the windows, and I am so accustomed to the homestead's big quiet that the motor in the room's tiny refrigerator unit sounds to me like a jackhammer. I am half tempted to slip back to the park where I'd napped.

In the morning I go down for the Welcome Breakfast and am—of course—early. I spend half an hour wandering campus, looking around at flowers and flyers, imagining the life of this place with students here.

Imagining students walking to class, so nervous, so hopeful, ready to try on their new lives and identities.

At the Welcome Breakfast, feeling hopeful myself, I put on a name tag and sit at a table with a fruit and cheese plate and make polite conversation with the fifty-year-old woman who sits beside me. She is wearing a taupe pantsuit, has big, curly brown hair. I'm in jeans and a T-shirt, and my hair hasn't been cut since I took some clippers to it back at the end of April. Yes, I'm excited to be here, I tell her. Yes, it is nice to see so many people come out in support of writing and writers. The small banquet hall is bright with sunlight, buzzing with excited talk. Looking around, I notice that most of the attendees are older than I am—two or three times older. The only other twentysomethings in the room are the university's uniformed waitstaff, offering people coffee.

This is my first clue that perhaps I have made a mistake coming here. The second is after we have all been welcomed by the conference director and sent to our classrooms and gotten settled in. For our first writing exercise, the instructor—the one I heard on the radio talking about the subject of place in fiction, a finalist one year for the National Book Award—splits the classroom into groups of three or four and asks us to talk about something painful in our lives, some painful memory. I am paired with two gentlemen forty years my senior, one of whom—a doctor from San Francisco—immediately starts in on a rant about how his ex-wife is taking him for everything he's worth. His money, his sailboat, his beloved dogs. The other gentleman is also from San Francisco, a banker. He tells about the death of his mother from some horrible disease, how he and his siblings had gone to war over their various inheritances. When it's my turn, the two of

Heat of the Summer

them look at me in my jeans and T-shirt, my wild hair. "What's he know about tough times?" the doctor jokes. "He's too young to have been through anything."

I am tempted to tell them how I've been living these last few months—out in a cabin with no electricity, no human contact. I am tempted to talk about my own divorce. But since they both talked about money, material things, I decide to tell them about the summer I spent working third shift at a factory. We made electric meters on a huge assembly line.

I worked a machine making a part for the meters called an overload. They looked like little jigsaw-puzzle pieces with copper bands in the middle and crimped tin edges. I had to stick my thumbs in the safety censors to engage the machine. In a series of lurching convulsions—the copper bar sucked up by a vacuum and dropped onto a pellet of olive-green glue onto the back of the piece of tin and crimped with a *ca-chunk*—the overload was put together and packed into a long tray. Across from my work station was an oven, where I'd bake the trays—forty-five minutes a tray at eight hundred degrees. Once they had cooled, another man on the assembly line would take them to his station and do with them whatever it was he did. I never found out what that was.

I never cared.

It was a monotonous job—a waste of human potential. But I was lucky. It was only for the summer. I met a woman there named Verna who'd been doing it for nineteen-some years. It was all she ever knew to do.

"Well, maybe he's been through a thing or two after all," the doctor says to the banker once I finish talking.

"Maybe so," the banker says.

I go through the motions of the class, eat lunch alone, and spend the rest of the afternoon at the pay phone chatting up my friends. But what is there to talk about that we didn't discuss yesterday? Back in my dorm room I tap away at my short story, annoyed by the buzzing drone of the fluorescent lights. That night, I go to a reading by my instructor, the finalist for the National Book Award a couple years back. It's nothing to write home about.

I don't want to judge everyone here by the doctor and the banker. There are surely some people in this crowd who care about writing, for whom writing is not just a pleasant leisure activity but a way of life. That's my attitude going into the second day. But when my class meets again it's more of the same—only this time it's two or three middle-aged women who dominate the class discussion, talking about agents, book contracts, and selling film rights (though, admittedly, none of them has written—much less published—a completed manuscript). And as I'm sitting there bored out of my skull, listening to this nonsense, it becomes clear to me: this isn't a writers' conference, it's a fantasy camp. You pay your money down, come to campus as part of a summer vacation, and for a week get to pretend you are America's next great literary voice. It sickens me—*sickens me*—that I have bought into such a scam.

The conference is set to last another three days, and I have a meeting scheduled with the National Book Award finalist at two o'clock this afternoon to talk about the first five pages of a story I sent in with my application—the story about the mother and the daughter and the thorns. But what is she really going to tell me that on some level I don't already know? Shit. I shouldn't have come.

After class, I head straight to my dorm room, pack up my clothes and laptop, and haul it all out to my truck. Just like that, in a matter of minutes, I'm on my way home to my little cabin along the Rogue.

I feel like a lover who's strayed and now wants to be taken back: I'm sorry, baby. I'll never leave again.

Heat of the Summer

I take the interstate north past Medford and Grants Pass, exit at Merlin, head west along the bumpy logging roads, following the BLM road numbers to the homestead. After three hours, I'm happily winding my way down the long drive. I pop the lock on the upper gate, slide through, and lock it behind me. Repeat the process at the lower gate. Drive past the pond, past the bench I made. And I think: This is where I want to be. *This is where I want to be!* At the lower house, I step out onto the deck. It is perfectly quiet this afternoon. The sun shines on Rattlesnake Ridge, hot air rippling off the rock. Why had I ever wanted to leave? What did I think was out there?

9

BIG AARON'S
VISIT

I'VE INVITED EVERY LAST ONE OF my friends to visit me in Oregon, but the only one who takes me up on it is Big Aaron. He's working on his master's degree in history back home at Purdue. This after a stint in politics at the Indiana statehouse, answering phones for Republican representatives and responding to their constituents' crazy e-mails and letters. To give an example: He heard from a woman complaining that the lottery was rigged. The odds on her scratch-off ticket said one in every five was a winner. She'd bought ten tickets but hadn't won at all. Shouldn't she have won twice?

Before politics Big Aaron's first job out of college (he was an economics major) was driving around to universities all across the country to give away dry-erase boards to students in return for their demographic information. There was an incident at UCLA, I believe, in which he was chased off campus.

Last winter, when I told Big Aaron of my plans to go it alone in Oregon, he said, "You can't do that. You're nuts."

Now it's August, and I'm at the little airport in Medford, waiting for his plane. Dave Reed from the BLM is waiting with me. In a show of generosity and kindness, Dave has volunteered to put us up—a couple of strangers—at his house for the night. Our plan is to get an early start tomorrow, drive to Crater Lake in the morning, and be back to the homestead by dark.

It has been nearly three months since I have seen a familiar face from back home, and when I catch a glimpse of Big Aaron coming down the terminal, a bag slung over his shoulder, I can't help but smile. We're going to have a good week: Crater Lake tomorrow and then five days at the homestead, drinking beer, barbecuing, hiking all around. That's the plan. I call his name and wave him over, give him a handshake, a hug. I introduce him to Dave Reed, who grins and then stands back a little, looks Big Aaron up and down, says I wasn't kidding about his being tall. At six-foot-six and with a head of honey-blond hair, Big Aaron most days resembles a grizzly standing on its hind legs to get a better look at something blurry in the distance. Today, however, he resembles a grizzly that's been tranquilized and is only now starting to come to. The flight from Indianapolis to Portland hadn't been terrible, but the flight from Portland to Medford was a roller coaster. He has the unmistakable look in the eye of someone who has recently tasted bile in the back of his throat. Dave and I take him outside for some fresh air.

It is another hot summer day, early August. A haze hangs over Medford. Out on one of the big hillsides north of the airport a wildfire is burning, and the three of us watch it. Roiling plumes of yellow-white smoke drift up into the sky, dissipate. Dave pulls a handkerchief from his pocket and wipes the back of his neck, says it's been burning since yesterday. Big Aaron says he could see it from the plane. I look at the fire, then at the ring of mountains. It's all so volcanic looking. Add the cars and buildings and people, and Medford reminds me of Bedrock from *The Flintstones*.

We follow Dave from the airport to his house, where he and his wife, Stephanie, take us in and treat us to a home-cooked meal, ice-cold bottles of Coors, and for dessert bowls of ice cream with fresh blackberries. Afterward, we sit in lawn chairs in Dave's backyard, visiting, late into the night.

"I forgot to tell you," Dave casually mentions. "On my way out last May—I saw a cougar. Running up the road."

"Where?"

"At the lower gate."

I know cougars are around—I know it intellectually. But this makes them real. The lower gate. Last May. As we keep talking about the homestead, the river, it's all I think about: a cougar at the lower gate.

The next morning Big Aaron and I thank Dave Reed for his hospitality and take off for Crater Lake under a beautifully blue Oregon sky. From Medford it's a drive of a couple hours northeast, the highway flanked by large stands of Oregon white oak and ponderosa pine. Crater Lake sits at six thousand feet above sea level, and steadily we climb: up, up, up. In the back of my truck I've stuffed the barn coat I haven't worn since spring. Dave said to make sure to bring it with me, because at six thousand feet Crater Lake could be chilly, even in the dead of summer. Chilly sounds good to me. Big Aaron, too. We roll down the windows, hang our arms out the sides.

As signs for the park appear, we follow them. After paying a ranger our entrance fee at the front gate and chatting with a bicyclist out for a spin, we drive up to the park's lodge on the edge of the caldera, slip out of the truck, and behold the lake itself, a massive quicksilver mirror some six and a half miles wide and nineteen hundred feet deep, reflecting a sky bulging with massive silver-blue clouds.

The water isn't the famous Crater Lake blue Dave had promised—as blue as the brightest blue sky—but it's still gorgeous. And at a cool fifty-seven degrees, I need my barn coat. Big Aaron puts on a heavy flannel.

I tell Big Aaron what I learned from a book in the homestead's library: the Rogue River's headwaters begin here.

From underground springs fed by cracks in the bedrock at the bottom of Crater Lake, where icy water continuously seeps into the earth, the river bubbles to the surface and races down the western slopes of the Cascades and into the Klamath Mountains, finding its own level in the Pacific.

We spend a couple hours scrabbling around the rim of the caldera, taking pictures of the sheer rock cliffs, gazing out at Wizard Island, pondering the volcanic eruption that obliterated Mount Mazama and left behind this huge serene-looking body of rainwater and snowmelt and the vast pumice desert that surrounds it. Then we decide to drive the thirty miles around the lake. No matter the angle of approach there's no shrinking this spectacle to a manageable scale. Crater Lake is enormous, the kind of natural wonder you could spend a lifetime pondering and still not understand. But all Big Aaron and I have is this one morning and a couple hours into the afternoon. So we drive around the caldera slowly, stopping from time to time to take more pictures, to look out at the pumice desert and the mountains in the distance. Once we've driven the entire thirty-mile circumference it's only with great reluctance that I signal and aim the truck west. We both wish we'd given ourselves longer here, but I promise Big Aaron that what's waiting for him at the homestead is every bit as wondrous.

On the long ride back to Grants Pass, Big Aaron stares out the window at the passing trees and the dipping power lines along the road. I watch the hazy shapes of mountains on the horizon. The closer we get to Grants Pass, the more traffic appears. Douglas firs give way to shabby houses, a railroad track, cars up on blocks in front yards, dusty corrals big enough for one horse. If not for the mountains and the dryness of the heat, we could be cruising through rural Indiana.

We take a late lunch at a Thai restaurant, then head to the grocery store for a week's worth of grub. The idea is not to eat but to feast. We buy noodles and cheap cuts of steak for Big Aaron's bourbon stroganoff and avocados, salsa, sour cream, and chicken to put on the tacos I plan on making.

We buy a case of Tecate.

Once everything's loaded into the back of the truck, we make one more quick stop at the post office, where I pick up a letter or two, and then we burn up the interstate to Merlin, wind our way to the homestead.

For the next two hours we don't see another vehicle, not one, just the skinny, bumpy logging road, extraordinary views down the river canyon, mountain on mountain. In my growing anxiety to be back before dark and get settled in for the week, I practically fly down the road. From the corner of my eye I catch Big Aaron gazing down uncertainly at the five hundred–foot drop-offs that so impressed my father and me back in April. He's got that green-in-the-gills expression he'd stepped off the airplane with yesterday, and I tell him there's nothing to worry about, I could drive this road blindfolded. Which is exactly when, taking one of the curves too fast, the truck fishtails in the gravel.

"Sorry about that," I say, laughing.

By the time we get to the homestead and slip through the gates, it's early evening, and both of us are exhausted. We unload our groceries, and I show Big Aaron around the cabin. It is just as Bradley's manual describes: small but comfortable. Big Aaron looks around at the cracked linoleum of the kitchen floor, at the frayed living room carpet. "It's a little rougher than I thought," Big Aaron says.

"What did you expect?"

We make dinner, and I take him to the upper house to watch the stars come out over Rattlesnake Ridge. The first stars hover just above the eastern horizon, flickering. Slowly, more and more pierce the dark.

Later, when we want to feel closer to everything—to the night sky, the stars—we walk down the drive a piece and lie on our backs in the powdery red dirt. Overhead the Milky Way is a vast pale splotch. Satellites slip by in their steady orbits. Shooting stars flare and dissolve. I remind Big Aaron of what Dave Reed said last night about seeing a cougar near the lower gate, tell him that Bradley saw one last summer running down this very driveway, chasing a black bear. Lying in the powdery red dirt, watching the stars, I realize that I'm part of that story now. Part of this place.

ONE OF THE THINGS I'VE LEARNED after four months alone is that when you live in solitude you forfeit the chance to serve others, to offer the kinds of small kindnesses that express your gratitude. So over the next few days, I take advantage of Big Aaron's presence and make him pancakes for breakfast, clean up his dishes afterward, and make sure he's got everything he needs to be comfortable. In the mornings we take it slow, staring out at Rattlesnake Ridge as the sun comes up and listening to the weather report on NPR. Here in southern Oregon there are about six different regions, whose weather on any given day could be completely different: the coast, the coast range, the north end of the valley, the south end of the valley, the Cascades, and, farther east, the high desert. At the homestead, however, the weather is unchanging: the temperatures rise into the triple digits by four o'clock every day, then fall off precipitously overnight.

Big Aaron's Visit

After breakfast I send Big Aaron to the upper house for a couple hours so I can get some writing done. He's glad enough to go. He's reading Shelby Foote's *Civil War: A Narrative*, and the view from the deck at the upper house is as spectacular as one could hope to find out here. Yes, it's hard for me to keep working with my friend around, with someone here to talk to, but the work of writing is why I've subjected myself to all this time alone. I've got to make the most of it.

Around ten or eleven, I head up to the upper house and find Big Aaron napping on a padded bench, his book on the floor. "Look at you," I tease him. "Loafing around like a bum. Asleep at the switch."

We slip down into the orchard below the upper house, explore bear trails that lead into the forest. We head up to the pond, and I show Big Aaron the bench I made, the cistern where our drinking water comes from, the newts at play. Every day it's something different but the same: We spend the hour or so before lunch just messing around. Then over lunch we start planning. What are we going to do today? What do we want to do? Depending on the heat and our general dispositions, we choose whatever sounds best. One day we hike to the river to go swimming. Another we pull out the homestead's 30.06 and set up a rifle range, blast to hell several rotten madrone rounds. Other suggestions are declined: Should we go to the coast and see the ocean, cool off? Should we drive up to the manzanita-choked Jeep road that leads to Rattlesnake Ridge and look for rattlesnakes? At the end of the day, regardless of our choices, we make our way back to the homestead and cook up a feast, drink a few beers, and afterward wade into the blackberry canes. The berries are big and plump, full of sun-warm juice. They break open in the mouth with only the slightest pressure from the tongue.

The day we decide to hike to Zane Grey's cabin, I willingly skip my morning writing so we can get started early. We pack a lunch (summer sausage, crackers, cubes of cheddar cheese) and fill several big bottles with water. It's an eight-mile hike round-trip, and with temps in the triple digits we're going to need every last drop. If it's not enough, I wouldn't feel too bad about drinking from one of the Rogue's burbling creeks, where the water comes gushing clean and cold over a bed of polished stones. But diarrhea brought on by giardiasis is not my idea of good times.

Water bottles in the backpack, we leave around nine or ten o'clock, skimming our way down the trail to the river. It's not yet hot, and in the forest's deep shade it almost feels cool. A dampness hangs in the air.

At the river we hike northwest, the morning sun on our backs. Steller's jays squawk from their low perches in a stand of madrones. Sunlight glimmers on the cliffs' chiseled undersides. Big Aaron asks me what I know about Zane Grey and his cabin, and I tell him I don't know much, just that he used to live here for a time, and, though I've not read the passages in question, he apparently wrote very movingly about the river. That's what the guide who'd taken my folks and me up the Rogue in a jet boat had told me last May. He also said Grey was a fantastic drunk who was forever having to be rescued after getting his boat hung up in the rocks. I've tried reading one of his westerns in the homestead's library but can't get past the first few pages. Call me a literary snob.

There is no road to Zane Grey's, only this trail and the river. Big Aaron and I, having taken our time in the heat, arrive shortly after noon. Our first signs of humanity are three big cisterns high up on one of the hills, like the one the Boydens use at the homestead, and the unmistakable tick of a sprinkler system. Another quarter mile and the little footpath we're following veers south and spits us out onto a huge, closely trimmed swatch of grass so green that it almost hurts my eyes.

To the west sits a modern ranch-style house and a garden

with several rows of eight-foot-tall sweet corn. The cabin is a stone's throw from the house. A little gray shack. Square. A couple of old windows. Big Aaron and I walk around it, take a peek inside, read through the names in the guest book, and sign it ourselves. All in all, it looks like a good place for a fiction writer to hole up.

After checking out the cabin, Big Aaron and I unpack our lunches and eat in the shade. A little tabby comes to join us, lolling on her side, licking a paw. "You're going to remember all this," I tell Big Aaron.

"Yeah?"

"Coming out here. The two of us."

Big Aaron thinks about it a second, takes a long drink of water, says he's glad he came. He asks if I'm ever going to come back to Indiana. I tell him I don't know. Then we're both quiet a moment. Big Aaron says, "It gets into you, doesn't it? I mean, I've only been here a week, and I feel it already."

On the hike back to the homestead that afternoon the temperature hits somewhere in the neighborhood of one hundred and eight. Heat radiates off the mountains in shimmering waves. The only things moving are the river and the turkey vultures, black specks in the sky above. To cool off before hiking the steep section of trail home, Big Aaron and I strip naked and jump in the river. The shallows are still warmish, but out more than a foot or two the water turns wonderfully, lung-tighteningly cool. To think of Crater Lake and the river's headwaters and all the little tributary creeks splashing down from springs in the mountains to create this coolness. And at the same time to think of nothing at all. To just swim, enjoy the water and the sunlight. There isn't a word I could write, even if I wrote for a thousand years, that could approximate this goodness: a wild river on a hot summer afternoon. Which is perhaps one of the paradoxes of being a writer: one's desire to fully inhabit one's life crashes like a wave against the desire to memorialize that life. Though they were obviously very different kinds of writers, and perhaps the most they ever had in common was the size of their cabins, Zane Grey and Henry David Thoreau, I'm sure, each felt a tension between their lives in the world and their lives on the page.

For Big Aaron and me on this summer's afternoon—after having finished a swim and gotten dressed and climbed onto some rocks above the river—memorializing comes in the form of stories from childhood, stories about our fathers. Big Aaron's father is a lawyer who farms on the side. He served in Vietnam, having joined the army in order to escape a backwater Indiana farm town and a family of ne'er-do-wells. He was a captain, worked as some kind of a journalist. Saw a lot of death. On the rocks above the river, Big Aaron tells me about a buddy of his father's. They were walking through this village and came across a young Vietnamese boy lying facedown in a ditch. Dead. The buddy grabbed the boy's arm to lift him up. The arm came right out of its socket. And later, when Big Aaron's father came home from the war, he stepped off the plane carrying a bottle of hooch and a lamp he bought in Thailand. Right away another GI offered to help him carry the lamp and the bottle. Big Aaron's father said, "I carried this shit halfway around the world. I can handle it from here."

"I remember this time we were raking leaves," Big Aaron says, grinning. "Me and my brothers and my dad. I was a kid."

They were raking leaves one day in autumn, raking big piles out to the side of the road. Out of nowhere, a yellow Camaro came screeching around a corner and blasted through the leaves, scattering them to the wind.

"Jesus," I say.

Big Aaron's laughing. "He said, 'Get in the car!'"

So Big Aaron and his two brothers dove into the car, and his father took off after the yellow Camaro. They finally caught up

Big Aaron's Visit

to it in a parking lot outside a drugstore. His father wasted no time pulling a crowbar from the trunk and walking over to the Camaro: two quick blows, and he bashed off its side mirrors.

It makes me think about when we used to keep rabbits. We kept a couple dozen rabbits in hutches out by our back shed. The idea was that we'd raise them to eat (since my father had given up hunting years before, after accidentally shooting his dog). We'd raise them to eat and maybe even sell the fur to somebody who could use it to make a pair of gloves or a cap. One day it came time to kill the rabbits, and I wanted to watch. My mother wasn't inclined to let me, but I begged her.

So we're out back, my father and me. He's wearing leather work gloves, holding a hammer. He's got a rabbit by the scruff of its neck, and its back legs are kicking against the air. He taps the rabbit with the hammer. Right on the head. A sound like a walnut falling out of a tree onto a concrete sidewalk.

He taps its head again.

The rabbit's legs stop kicking. From the tender pink of its ear a slow line of blood begins to trickle out. The blood is thick like molasses, drips onto the ground, is absorbed. And that's all the more I remember.

Sitting on the rocks above the river, drying off after a swim, a steep climb up the trail home awaiting us, Big Aaron and I are loath to move. We tell a few more stories, stare at the water. I think about the little boy I used to be, the one who wanted to watch his father kill those rabbits. I think about how in the bathtub that night, with the same hand that had held the hammer, my father took a washcloth to my face and gently swabbed it clean. That sweet little boy. Day by day his life became the one I know now, the one where I'm caretaker of a backcountry homestead, living and writing in unparalleled solitude. It's a life I could never have even begun to imagine a year ago. Which makes me wonder what else is in store for me, who else I'll become, what it all will or won't mean. Today I sit with Big Aaron, and we watch the river.

BIG AARON'S LAST NIGHT AT THE HOMESTEAD. Having finished all our beer, we pour glasses of George Dickel, drop in ice cubes and sprigs of mint from the garden, and head to the upper house to watch the sun go down over the river canyon. It's been a full week: hiking, swimming, shooting guns. One night Big Aaron dreamed of human-sized newts dressed in tuxedos. One morning he woke up with a spider on his hand. We have cooked big meals and feasted and drunk beer. We've told stories, told lies, argued about politics. Now it's all coming to an end, and nostalgia's setting in.

The sky fades from pale blue to orange to pink. The mountains go green, reddish brown, black. On the sides of the upper house, from under the cedar shakes, hundreds of bats begin to scratch to life. Big Aaron and I sip our whiskey as they make their first tentative orbits around the deck, skimming mosquitoes and moths. A few stars appear in the gray air over Rattlesnake Ridge.

Perhaps because we've been talking about childhood this week, or because in one way or another the remoteness of the homestead invites such speculation, our talk turns to the question of life after death.

Big Aaron wants to believe that his soul somehow lives on. He wants to believe that life isn't accidental.

I want to believe that, too—I want to believe that there is some larger story we're part of, that someday our lives will make sense. But I have to ask him what exactly he finds so offensive about dying. "Is dying any different than before you were born? Were you sad before you were born?"

"It's different."

"Why?"

"Because I'm here now."

Big Aaron's Visit

When he asks me what I think happens after death, I say something that surprises me, something I haven't consciously thought of before but must have been brooding over because I say it with conviction, and after I've said it I won't back down. I tell Big Aaron that if there is something called a soul it's never ours but rather something we share with everyone else, the deer, the lizards, the rocks. All he has is his body and this moment, and after death his body will decompose and feed the earth the way a dead tree in the forest decomposes and feeds the earth. Should he expect anything different of a soul? Should he want anything different? We're down to the wilted mint leaves in our drinks. It's dark. Bats circle the cabin, snagging moths attracted by the wall lamps. Big Aaron tells me I'm crazy, I'm drunk. I tell him neither of those things makes me wrong.

PREMONITIONS

MID-AUGUST THE MADRONES LOSE THEIR leaves and start growing new ones—a broadleaf evergreen. I've never heard of such a thing and am amazed. Just as I am amazed by the ferocity of the yellowjackets now that we're on the cusp of autumn. In the garden they swarm the windfall apples, boring down for sweetness. When I toss a sharp rock into the river and cut my finger, a pair of them arrive within seconds to lap the drops of blood that fall. In the mornings I like to stand on the deck and watch them spark to life from a nest under the cabin, their hollow bodies filling with light.

On one such morning a strange thought occurs to me: I should go to the garden, pick a few apples, and take them to some hikers along the river. This is a strange thought because even though a backpacking trail follows the Rogue, I have yet to see a single hiker in the five months I've lived here.

But what the hell? I grab my backpack and a water bottle, hit the garden, pick three Golden Delicious apples.

Down at the river the water is purling, glassy, deep green (almost black) in the morning sun. Somewhere upstream a water ouzel is singing. John Muir's favorite bird. I hike northwest and climb out onto some steep-sharp metamorphic rocks and watch the sun come up over the canyon. A few early-bird rafters splash by with waves of greeting, but I don't meet any hikers. After another half hour I head for a beach I like. In a cool spot in the shade, I lie down for a nap, and when I wake up it's coming on noon. Convinced of my folly in packing apples for three nonexistent hikers, I grab one from my pack and eat it, thinking of the day ahead, what's next.

And just about the time I stand up, ready to head home, I see them: hikers, three of them. A mother, a father, and their teenage son, fifteen miles into their excursion and lugging bulky forty-pound backpacks.

They have lost their trail map and want to know if I'm familiar with this part of the river, if I know a good spot nearby to camp for the night. I tell them that this beach is the best place to make camp unless they want to hike another five miles, and that not too much farther down the trail, perhaps a day's walk, is the Rogue River Ranch, a BLM holding where they can get a new map. The father notices that I've only got a day pack and asks me where I'm staying. I tell them I'm caretaking nearby and offer up the apples I picked. They take them somewhat warily, but soon enough, enticed by the oncoming afternoon heat and the prospect of another lunch of dry beef jerky, they are all three crunching away. We talk a few minutes more, and I wish them luck on the hike. They thank me for the apples.

On the steep climb up the mountain home, sweating, panting,

pausing from time to time to glance across the sun-dappled forest floor and up into the blue sky, I have no need to explain how I knew I'd meet these people. I thought maybe I'd pick some apples and give them away. What could be more ordinary?

The true marvel is how the afternoon sun feels on my skin, how the quiet of the homestead—a quiet that contains the buzzing yellowjackets and the river crashing against its boulders—stills my unquiet mind. The true marvel is the realization that comes to me a few days after having given apples to the hikers: the only way to be worthy of the gift of my time at Dutch Henry is to leave the homestead in better shape than I found it, that what I have to give to this place is more important than what I take away.

IN THIS GENEROSITY OF SPIRIT I start working on the trail to the river, cutting back weeds with a shovel. When the fall steel-head run is in full effect come September, I want Bradley and Frank and whoever else may arrive with fish on the brain to have a clear path. I use the shovel like a scythe and swat the weeds. After a summer of drought—it has not rained an inch since late May—the weeds crumble at the slightest touch. It's dry, dusty work. Three straight afternoons I eat my lunch, head down the trail, spend an hour or two bent over the shovel.

By the end of the third day, after three hours in the heat, I find myself in the big meadow where we'd seen a herd of two dozen deer in April. The grass is tall and brittle, blowing around in a hot breeze.

One of the books in the homestead's library, a chronicle of the Rogue Indian War, mentions that this meadow was for a time the site of a militia encampment. Now there's just wind, a barbed-wire fence blistered with rust.

I look around at the grasses, the flowering bull thistle, and try to imagine what this place must have looked like crawling with men and horses and livestock. Did they eat hot meals here, take shits in the woods, shoot their guns, cheat at cards, drink too much (or not enough) whiskey, miss their mothers, wives, and children? And what about the Rogue River Indian peoples? I don't know how to think about their lives. The silence I've known at the homestead—which has gotten inside me, split my heart open like a melon—was theirs for thousands of years before the Europeans arrived. Do their spirits still inhabit this place?

Back at the cabin, at the end of a long day, I clean up and poke around the kitchen for something to eat. It's been more than a week since I've gone to town and gotten groceries. The cupboard is bare. I have some just-add-water pancake mix, but that would require me to wash a bowl and a spoon, because over the last week I've let the dishes pile up in the sink. Laziness. And just-add-water pancakes—they are so thin and familiar (I eat them two or three times a week)—don't sound good.

So I decide not to eat: I'm going to town tomorrow, I'll just get something then. For now I crack open a book.

I've only barely gotten started reading, however, when I hear voices. It occurs to me that there are guns in the closet behind the hot water tank, that maybe I should grab one. But I check myself: do you really want to shoot someone tonight? I take a deep breath and step onto the deck.

Down at the head of the trail to the river stand two grown men, in their fifties or older, and what look like their two teen-age sons. One of them is pointing toward the barn and talking quietly. I call out to them.

The four look up, and the one who had been talking and gesturing toward the barn says, "Don't let us disturb you."

Don't let us disturb you? You're trespassing on a backcountry homestead two hours from town and I haven't seen any other human beings in at least eight days—and you tell me I shouldn't be disturbed? "Well, let me at least come down and meet you," I say, deciding to leave the 30.06 in the closet.

Premonitions

We meet at the bottom of the turnaround. The man who didn't want to disturb me is tall and thin, decked out in khaki from head to toe—khaki pants, vest, and hat—with close-cropped hair turning silver on his sideburns. He introduces himself and produces a business card from his wallet. His name is Ogden Kellogg Jr. and he's a retired agricultural extension agent from Oregon State University. He introduces me to his son and his friend and his friend's nephew. We all shake hands. They have been floating the river, Ogden says. It's something he's been doing since he was five, when his grandfather first took him along. "That was with Glen Wooldridge," he says.

Anyone familiar with the Rogue and its history as a white-water rafting river will know the name Glen Wooldridge. I read about him in a book in the homestead's library. He was the first to travel from Grants Pass to Gold Beach in a wooden boat. And years later, rather than portage, he would dynamite any stone riffle in his way. In such a manner he opened the Rogue for river traffic and became its most famous guide.

It was from Ogden Kellogg Jr.'s river trips with his grandfather and Wooldridge that he knew of the Dutch Henry Homestead, and in particular the barn, its last remaining structure from the gold-mining days. And because he and his party climbed a steep and muscle-numbing trail at the end of what was already a long, hot day of rafting to see a hand-hewn hundred-year-old barn, because his friend has pulled a camcorder from his backpack and is panning all around in wonder, because the two boys, both of them sixteen or seventeen, are looking around and loving the idea of this hideaway in the woods, I'm not inclined in the least to ask them to leave. Instead we all talk a while about Glen Wooldridge and the story of Dutch Henry, who killed two of his business partners (one of whom he tossed in the river, whose corpse later turned up stinking and bloated in Gold Beach). I offer to show them around the property. We go to the barn, the garden, and to the upper house, where we stand in awe of the view from the deck. They envy me my quiet life here, and I envy them their companionship, their journey down the river. Someday, I tell them, I want to hike the whole thing.

Later, the afternoon giving way to evening, Ogden asks me if I have had dinner yet and tells me they met some fishermen on the river today who had caught a thirty-seven-pound salmon.

"They gave us more than we can carry in our cooler," he says. "If you want, you can come down and get some."

I don't tell them that just before they arrived I had decided not to eat dinner at all, that nothing sounded good, but as I follow them down the trail—the shadows of the big Doug firs stretching long and black as the sun begins to wane—it's all I can think about. Last week there were some hikers to whom I gave apples. This week, when I decide not to eat, a meal comes to me. It feels like more than coincidence, but I don't know what to call it. Karma? Serendipity? Or maybe this is how the world always has worked, but I'm just now noticing it. Just now starting to pay attention.

Down at the Rogue the sun has dipped below the western peaks, and the water has gone black. The boys rip off their T-shirts and sandals and cannonball from a rock into the river. Ogden fills a plastic sack with three chunks of bright-pink salmon, and I half consider asking him if I can hang around, sleep down here tonight. The thought of lying on this beach with the river lapping up onto the rocks, stars freewheeling overhead in their shimmering constellations; the thought of joining not only Ogden and his rafting party but the quiet that surrounds us, the purling water, the insects, the wing beats of bats beginning to flutter in the treetops—it pulls at me, as though the quiet is its own river, steadily dissolving my small, scared self. Yet as tempting as it is to stay, I want to get an early start to town tomorrow. I want to talk to my people. So I thank everyone for the salmon and head

Premonitions

home feeling happy for how the day has ended, for the gift of food when I was hungry. Still, there is another part of me—call it intuition, conscience—that knows I have passed up an opportunity to give myself more fully to this river canyon. A doorway had opened to me, and, for some reason, I chose not to enter.

Days later I'm writing a letter at my chipped breakfast table, describing to a friend just how delicious was the salmon Ogden and his rafting party gave me, when I hear the rustle of a big animal in the tall grass behind the garden. Too big to be Cougar-Bait or one of his buddies. I grab my binoculars and slip outside as quietly as possible. Only a bear could make a sound like that. Lumbering. Brushy. My truck is parked in the driveway in front of the deck, and I crouch behind it, look out at the garden and beyond. At first all I see are the apple trees, yellow apples hanging in the branches, the leaves beginning to curl and dry up. Then I spot the bear. It's sitting in the grass like a giant field mouse. It looks in my direction but doesn't appear to see me. I bring the binoculars to my eyes. At a distance of less than a hundred yards, separated only by the garden fence and a stand of apple trees, the bear is suddenly enormous. It's eating windfall apples I tossed out for the deer. It picks one up with its lips and front teeth—a softball-sized Golden Delicious—and with a flip of the head drops the apple into the back of its mouth and crunches it down in three quick bites. It does this again and again. Four apples in less than a minute. The bear is so goddamn near in the binoculars I can see the reddish hairs on its back, the doglike wetness of its nose. The bear is so beautiful that the breath goes out of me, and I have to pull the binoculars away. My heart is beating in my throat. When finally the wind shifts and carries my scent across the garden, the bear stands perfectly still a moment. It lifts its nose in my direction, searchingly, suspiciously, and flexes its wet black nostrils, sniffs the air. One long draft, then another, and in an instant—its suspicions confirmed—the bear turns tail and lopes off into the forest. Afterward, scanning the tree line for movement, I marvel at the bear's speed and power. I walk down to the garden and grab a few more big windfalls and toss them into the meadow where the bear had been feeding. *Come back, come back.*

THE NEXT MORNING I LISTEN to the radio—a BBC feed that the local NPR affiliate has switched to—and look out at the mountains, at Rattlesnake Ridge, everything so very still in the dawn's first light. There is apparently some confusion in the reporting: a plane has hit a building; no, two planes. And since it's the BBC, I think that a plane must have crashed somewhere in England and feel a pang of sympathy when I hear about the second plane. How awful for those poor people, I think. Yet I still can't understand why NPR would switch over from American news to cover such a thing.

I make my breakfast like any morning: a bowl of cereal, a banana. Something the reporter says catches my attention. New York. Washington DC. Pennsylvania. As many as four planes. I put down my spoon.

Out on the deck in my shirtsleeves, I look around. A robin, perched on the barn roof, lets out its single piercing chirrup. All down the river canyon, a smoky white fog—in giant flame-shaped wisps—rises through the Douglas firs just as it has on September mornings for thousands of years. Nothing here has changed in the slightest. But then I realize. Every clear morning for the past five months, I have looked out at the sky over Rattlesnake Ridge and seen a pair of jet contrails—two perfect white lines stretching from horizon to horizon. This morning all U.S. domestic flights have been grounded. The sky is empty. My only proof the news is real.

I have a satellite phone for emergencies and use it to call

my friend Michelle back home in Indiana. She is nine months pregnant now and due to deliver in the next week or so. It is also her birthday.

"This is the world I'm bringing my baby into," she says. "What the fuck's going on? Seriously. What the fuck?"

We talk only briefly, because the satellite phone costs a dollar or two a minute. Afterward, I turn the radio back on and listen until the batteries run down and the station crackles out. Then it's too quiet in the cabin. I sit in my truck and listen to the radio—the same story looped over and over. NPR correspondents in New York are on bicycles, reporting what they see and have seen. The soot and stink and death. People leaping out high windows. The sickening explosion of the second plane. Eventually, because I can't afford to waste gas or run down the battery in my truck, I switch it off, and the quiet returns.

Over the next few hours, I try to make myself useful and end up in the garden, down in the dirt, pulling weeds from the strawberry beds. Since there is no one around to talk to, I talk to the terrorists. "You think this changes anything, you stupid, stupid motherfuckers? Now all that's going to happen is . . ." and I get quiet, heartsick. Already I know. Our national response to this tragedy will be more tragedy, more bloodshed, and it will find its way—because it always finds its way—to those innocent of any crime, to children, to the poor. It doesn't take any special clairvoyance to realize that this day will stretch out over the coming weeks and months like the skin of a drum, and that we will pound it.

On September 12, I make the trip to town. I listen to radio coverage the whole two hours, everything still fresh, raw. Occasionally, a view opens up on the road ahead and stretching to the horizon—as though the work of some enormous raging tornado—the timber-slashed hillsides lie in wrack and ruin from a clear-cut. It's not the first time I've noticed the practice and felt a pang of despair, but it seems worse this morning.

I cross a bridge over the Rogue and slip through Merlin, where at the gas station someone has hung a big cardboard sign that reads: NO GAS. I don't understand. Up the interstate a few miles in Grants Pass, all the gas stations have similar signs. It doesn't dawn on me what's happened, that in the wake of yesterday's news everyone has filled up their tanks, fearing the worst. As I drift farther into town, I see American flags waving on car antennas and hanging off front stoops and lowered to half-mast in front of schools and fire stations. Everywhere I look there is shock and sadness, strangers talking to each other on the sidewalks, shaking their heads. At the Fred Meyer grocery store, where I stop to use the pay phone and pick up some groceries, a man I don't know holds the door open for me.

I call my parents, who had been watching FOX News just after the first plane hit and had seen the second one come screaming in. They are still in shock. "We just thought it was a Piper Cub or something," my mother says. "We were having our coffee, watching the news. Then here comes the second one."

"Boom," my father says.

"Jesus," I say.

We talk and talk and talk. They had wondered if I'd heard the news. My mother says there's no more gas in Lafayette. I tell her there's no more gas here, that I'm glad my truck has a thirty-gallon tank. Just day-to-day concerns. We don't talk about the death and destruction and how terrible it is. We know that it is terrible.

After chatting with my folks, I make a few more calls. My friend Patricia shares my fears about our response to this tragedy, and as we are talking—as we are hoping that cooler heads will prevail in Washington—I hear the man on the pay phone next to me describing in detail what he would do to Osama Bin Laden if he could get his hands on him. "We just need to go over there and have ourselves a throat-slitting party," he says. Then he hangs up and strolls out to his car in the parking lot, disappears into a

Premonitions

snarl of traffic. It's only now I realize that the man who wants to go over there and have a throat-slitting party is the same man who held the door open for me.

After phone calls and groceries and a stop at the post office to gather my mail, I have one last errand in town before the two-hour slog back to the homestead. The Silver Sedge Fly Shop in Merlin. The Rogue's autumn halfpounder steelhead run is about to commence, and I have precious little knowledge in terms of flies, leaders, and so forth. I've been told that the owner of The Silver Sedge, Rusty, is a master fly tier, a sage of the river, the man to talk to if you want to catch a fish. It's true that I'd rather chat him up and introduce myself under better circumstances, but this is my one trip to town for the next week or two. He's back behind the counter when I walk in, tying a fly, a pair of glasses on the very tip of his nose. He's an old man, anyone's gray-headed grandfather, with a beer gut and a big bulbous nose, an inky tattoo of an anchor on his forearm. There is a portable TV in the corner, and the news is on. He's tying flies, watching the news. His eyes are red-rimmed, weary. I pick up a few items, lay them on the counter, and he rings me up without looking away from the television. I tell him I'm caretaking along the Wild and Scenic section of the Rogue. He grunts. It's not until I ask if he has any suggestions in terms of fishing for steelhead that he seems to notice me. "Uh, well, you know," he says in a gravelly voice. "Sometimes you catch 'em. Sometimes you don't." I pay in cash, and he hands me my change. On the two-hour trip back to the homestead I keep seeing his red-rimmed eyes, his anchor tattoo. It comes to me that perhaps he is a veteran of World War II or Korea, that maybe he thought he'd seen the end of this kind of thing.

THE NEXT THREE DAYS AT the homestead are a blur. I have new batteries for my radio and spend hour after hour listening to the news, trying to get a sense of what has happened and what we're going to do about it. There are stories about the missing, about victims and their families. If anything is a comfort it's the thought that this world of ours—the kind of world in which such a tragedy could happen—is also the one its victims loved. It is the world that the rest of us, the survivors, must now try to love again the rest of our lives, if only for the sake of those so unfairly taken away.

Then on the fourth or fifth morning afterward, it occurs to me: all of these things I've been thinking, these grand thoughts of love and death, war and peace, are just that, thoughts. I have been snagged by my thoughts just as surely as a bat snags a moth. I get up and go to the radio but don't turn it on. Instead I step out onto the deck, look up at the sky over Rattlesnake Ridge.

The jet contrails have returned.

And somehow I return.

I pack a lunch and head down to the river with my fly rod and the special flies Rusty at the Silver Sedge tied for me. I spend the morning fishing, practicing my cast from the top of a boulder. I let out plenty of line with my left hand and then wheel the rod back in my right, shoot it forward, and send the fly skimming out across the water. I'm no artist, and the sunlight does not refract off of my line in glitzy, radiant arcs. Rather, I struggle. My fly gets tangled in the willows behind me. I cast knots in my line. All morning, I don't turn a single fish. But neither am I discouraged, because I'm at the river and the river is beautiful: its fish smell, its coolness, glassy green water sloshing gray metamorphic rock, the sky reflected on the water's surface. At noon, I take a break and eat lunch in the shade of a river oak and think about the hikers I gave some apples to, the bear I saw, the attacks on the World Trade Center and the Pentagon. Thoughts come and go, and I let them come and go. There is nothing to gain from holding on to them.

Premonitions

AFTERSHOCKS

ONE WEEK AFTER THE ATTACKS, I make another trip to town for another round of phone calls, groceries, laundry, and mail. Only this time at the grocery store, before getting a cart and stuffing it full of food and supplies, I walk straight to the magazine racks and open up a *Newsweek*. Here is proof: black smoke roiling from the towers; screaming, dust-covered men and women gazing up in horror as the second plane comes in; the scattered remains of Flight 93 in Pennsylvania; the smoldering crater at the Pentagon. Most everyone else has been watching the footage on television, living with the images for a week now. This is my first real exposure. The photos hit with the force of a blow to the solar plexus. I stand in the aisle at the grocery on the verge of tears over the terrified Asian American in his dust-covered navy-blue business suit, running down a crowded New York sidewalk, his briefcase flying out at his side. And I pity the young Palestinian boy pictured in another of the magazines: he's no more than eight or nine years old and is firing a machine gun into the air. Someone has told him it's a time to celebrate. Now is no time for anyone to celebrate.

Even my friend Michelle, whose first child is due to be born in another week, is not celebrating. When I talk to her on the phone she is scared about the kind of world her son will be born into. Is there going to be a war? Will he have to fight? How can she protect him from a violence so out of the blue?

When I talk to Big Aaron, he tells me that on the flight home from Oregon he realized he had spent rifle shells in his pants pockets from the homestead's 30.06. "Why didn't security stop me?" he says.

My parents have been glued to the news and tell me stories about the firefighters who charged up the stairwells as the towers collapsed, about who the government thinks is responsible. Then they tell me more local news, about a prayer vigil at church, about price gouging at the gas pumps. My mother thinks that the jet contrails she saw late on the afternoon of the eleventh must have been the president's, flying back to Washington from Iowa or wherever he was taken after news of the attacks.

All the way home that afternoon, I think about my people—my mother and father, Big Aaron, Michelle. I think about how lucky I am to know them, to love and be loved by them. It is a strange time to feel grateful, after the tragedies in New York, Washington DC, and Pennsylvania, but selfishly I do. And though it is terrible to say, I feel grateful no one I know was killed. It's how I imagine many people are feeling—strangely and sadly relieved. Yet any portion of relief is paid for with the dread knowledge that it could have just as easily been you and your family. On the phone something my mother said stuck with me: "Maybe next they'll take out a small town like ours—poison the drinking water, who knows—just to show they can. Then wouldn't anybody feel safe."

That she would even think of such a thing means she already feels unsafe. It's an aftershock from the attacks.

As for me, driving these winding backcountry logging roads, looking out at the mountains, the river, I'm not scared at all. It is a complete reversal from this spring, when the indifference of the landscape felt somehow ominous and cruel. Now the indifference is a comfort. It doesn't matter what happens to human beings, how we kill each other—not to the mountains. Their mystery will survive.

Maybe because of all this, because I'm feeling so enlightened by my days along the river; or because I'm full of pity and love and sadness for the people in the magazines at the grocery store; because my mother is afraid; because Michelle is having her baby; because I know that in two months I will be leaving Oregon and returning to Indiana, where the only wilderness is in one's mind; maybe because of all this, when I meet up with two men on the road near the homestead in a white pickup truck with some kind of official-looking decal on the door, I greet them as friends. They are wearing khaki shirts. Some kind of uniform. Our trucks pull up window to window, and the driver—twenty-four years old, perhaps, with a goatee and sunglasses and skull tattoos scrolling up both his arms—says they are from a fire crew ten miles downriver. They want to know if I am the homestead's caretaker, and without even thinking about it—because I should just tell them that I'm only out for a scenic drive, because nobody needs to know my business but me—I tell them, yes, I'm the caretaker. The driver wants to know if they can come see the homestead's pond. And because I've greeted them as friends, I say sure, why not, and they turn around and follow me down the homestead's bumpy driveway.

We slip through the upper and lower gates, and I show them the pond. They get out of the truck, look at it. It looks fine. Afterward, since there's not a good place to turn around by the pond, I have them follow me to the cabins. And because it hasn't been that long since Ogden and his rafting party came to visit, and because that generosity on my part had resulted in a few big salmon steaks, I invite the men from the fire crew down to the garden for some ripe Concord grapes. We stand in the garden picking grapes and popping them into our mouths and spitting the seeds. The one with the skull tattoos down his arm does all the talking.

"My grandfather logged these hills," he says, motioning around at the mountains. "My great-grandfather was a miner."

He's looking around at the grapevines in the garden, the apple trees, the barn, and up to the lower house with its big deck and its blue propane pig in the side yard. I ask him what he does in the winter when there isn't any need for a fire crew downriver. He flips his aviator sunglasses onto the bill of his cap.

"Mount Ashland," he says.

"Mount Ashland?"

"Ski resort."

He says he works the summer out here on the fire crew, takes a month off, and starts at the ski resort for the winter. Another month off in the spring, and it's time get out to the fire crew again. They were out this way not too long ago, he says, doing trail maintenance in full fire gear. He pops a grape into his mouth, pushes it around with his tongue, and spits out the seeds. His companion, a big, quiet bear of a man, standing cross-armed and bored, looks at the ground, says nothing.

"So you're from Indiana?" the one with the tattoos says, brushing grape skins off his hands, then wiping his hands on his pants. "You have a relative here or something?"

"The closest person I know," and I try to calculate the miles to Dave Reed's house, "is maybe seventy miles."

"You're alone?"

"Yeah."

"See many deer?"

I tell him I see deer every day, and he wants to know if any of them have any size. I shrug, tell him not really. I don't want him getting the idea that this would be some kind of great place to sneak into and poach a buck. He motions to his companion, says he's a big hunter. I ask the companion what he hunts.

"Elk," he says. "Bear."

"Big gun?" I say.

"30.06."

The one with the tattoos points to the head of the trail, says it looks like a good path to the river, and wants to know about the fishing. I tell him they're not biting yet or else I'm not a good-enough fly fisherman to catch them. He shakes his head, says he never got interested in fly fishing. Too many knots and too much fussing around with flies and leaders. Better, in his opinion, just to get a casting rod and throw out a spoon. And because we are talking fishing, because we have been standing in the garden for what is beginning to feel like an uncomfortably long time, because my heart is full with the tragedy of 9/11, because it's been so long since I've talked face-to-face with anyone and can't for the life of me just politely ask these two to leave, I start walking to my pickup and tell them that they should come back sometime later in the season and we can all take the trail to the river, spend an afternoon steelhead fishing.

And as soon as I've uttered the words I know that this is wrong, that it's in direct violation of the most fundamental rule Bradley sets down in the homestead manual: keep this place private.

The one with the tattoos wants to know how they can get ahold of me to set it up. I don't want to give them the number of the satellite phone because I don't want them to call. But I don't want them to just show up, either.

I give them the number.

"You know anything about the place next door?" the one with the tattoos says, glancing east, pointing.

He's referring to an unoccupied survivalist compound a few miles down the road. It's a castlelike building with a big tower and several gun turrets. Joe Green showed me a photo of it in the spring and admonished me never to go over there unless I wanted to get shot.

"We got a key," he says.

"To the house?"

"To the BLM gate."

He says it's a master key to all BLM gates. He says they may have to go back there and check out the compound. Then he and his companion climb into their rig and fire up the engine. I tell them I'm going to follow them out, lock up behind them, but the one with the tattoos on his arms waves me off, says they can take care of it from here. He holds up the paper with the number for the satellite phone, promises to be in touch about that fishing trip. They wave good-bye and head up the road.

I spend the hour after they've gone putting away my groceries and every so often checking the window. They could come back—there's nothing stopping them. Why am I so stupid? I can't understand it. And it's not just that I've broken the rules by inviting them back to go fishing. It's not just that I've told them how alone I am here. It's that they have a master key to the upper gate. Which wouldn't be so bad except for the fact that the lower gate—the one I'd beaten on with a chunk of wood my first day here alone—hasn't worked for the past month. The tongue no longer fits in its groove. Maybe because of how I'd beaten it. But the point is that they could come back. Hell, if they wanted, they could come in with a couple of rifles, take my truck, and load it up with everything at the homestead—the generator, the guns—and leave me for dead. They could be in Mexico by the time anybody even found me. And that's why Bradley's rule about keeping the homestead a secret from outsiders is so important, because the more people who know about the place, the greater the invitation to danger.

After an hour or two, I get in my truck and head up the driveway. The lower gate is closed as best as it can close, and the upper gate is locked. The men from the fire crew are nowhere to be seen. I slip through the upper gate, drive to the top of the road. No one's around. Just an empty late-afternoon forest.

What the hell was I thinking?

That night, I lie in bed remembering a story Joe Green had told that first weekend. A couple of teenagers had shot and killed the owner of a nearby lodge on one of these backcountry logging roads.

All night long I can barely sleep. I start thinking that the men from the fire crew with their master key could be out there right now, waiting until it got later, got darker. Then they could creep down with rifles and kill me, steal my truck. Or if not the men from the fire crew, then someone else, maybe someone they'd talked to. Maybe they got back to the fire lookout and started talking about this fool who lived all alone and didn't know anybody for seventy miles. Maybe someone else had gotten the idea to come in and shoot me, steal my truck. Maybe it's all happening now.

In the morning, instead of going down to the garden and watering the fruit trees, eating handfuls of grapes—a routine I've gotten into—I stay inside. I listen to the radio. Do my writing. Afterward, I crack open a book on the deck and read for several hours. Somehow the day passes without my ever having left the cabin. In the growing dark after dinner, I sit on the deck listening for the sound of crunching tires on the road, footsteps in the woods. When it's full dark and time to go to bed I load my day pack with a change of clothes, some food and water, the satellite phone. If they come for me in the night, I'll be ready. I'll slip out of the cabin and into the forest and disappear.

In case I don't wake up in time, I lay the homestead's .22 in bed beside me, scatter a handful of bullets beside my water glass on the nightstand. Now that I'm ready, I almost want them to come. I dare them.

But no one comes.

I lie in bed imagining scenarios in which I am some kind of Rambo stalking these assholes who've come to kill me.

In the middle of the night I wake up with a pounding heart and reach for the .22 and lie perfectly still, listening. Locusts buzz in nearby trees. Seconds pass. I relax my grip on the gun, close my eyes.

At first light I'm woken again, this time by footsteps right outside my bedroom window. The crunch of stepped-on madrone leaves, madrone leaves brushed aside by a slowly lifted foot. I lie stiff as a board, waiting. The sound gets closer and closer, and a face suddenly appears in the window: a black-tailed deer, picking through the briars, eating grass. It's so quiet, I hear his chewing.

When Bradley shows up a couple days later, I don't tell him about the guys from the fire squad or my freak-out. I don't want him to know how badly I've screwed up. There's enough to talk about anyway. When I spot him scurrying down the long dirt driveway, fly rod in hand, he calls out to me: "Suicide bombers!" On the mile-long trek to the river to go fishing it's all we talk about. A gorgeous, hot early-fall afternoon, sunlight dazzling the high traces of Douglas fir and ponderosa pine, we speak of New York, DC, the field in Pennsylvania. Bradley says he's glad we have a war hawk in the White House, then thinks better of it, shrugs. We head for "the platforms," Bradley's favorite fishing spot, flat rock cliffs twenty feet above the river, where you cast your fly into deep-green billowing pools, where the steelhead hover by the dozen, waiting for a meal. In the spring, he'd hooked a gorgeous sixteen-incher here and landed it by lying belly-down on the rock and quickly, hand over hand, retrieving his line.

By the time we arrive this afternoon, it is still too early to fish. The shadow of the western cliffs hasn't yet crossed the river channel, and steelhead won't take a fly in direct sunlight. Too many raptors. So we climb up the mountain a few hundred feet and sit in a clearing, gazing down at the water. Bradley says he just can't imagine what would propel someone to crash an airplane into a building like that.

"What would you die for?" I ask him.

"Nothing."

"Nothing at all?"

Then he thinks about it.

"Native steelhead," he says. "So my kids can love them as much as I do."

"Yeah?"

"Native steelhead."

Only something like 30 to 40 percent of all the steelhead in the Rogue are wild—most are born and raised in captivity, farmed, and they've got the clipped adipose fin to prove it. To the State of Oregon it is a fineable offense to keep a wild fish; to Bradley, sacrilege. The fish is the embodiment of the river and his love for the river, his memories of childhood, of everything worth passing on to the next generation.

"Always check for that clipped fin," Bradley says, looking at me over his shoulder. "I don't care how hungry you are—you could be starving to death for all I care—you don't keep the wild ones."

But it's only a day or two after Bradley's visit, after our conversation on the side of the mountain, waiting for a shadow to cross the river, that I catch a steelhead and, in my haste, bonk it on its head and put it in my creel without first checking the fin. As soon as I realize my mistake I know it will be a native (even though in twenty or thirty catches none have been native). And I am right. I check my creel, and there with its adipose fin perfectly intact is a fish for whom my friend Bradley would give his life. Maybe, I think, the fin hadn't been properly clipped at the farm. Maybe it grew back. Maybe I should cut it off with my fillet knife in case any Department of Fish and Wildlife guys show up. If no one else knows what I have done, I reason, has it even really happened? But the fish knows the truth, and so does the river. And so do I. Eventually. I take the fish to the water's edge and cut off its head and disembowel it, scraping my thumbnail over the knobs of its spine. I hold the fillet in the river and let the current rinse it clean. Then I climb up the mountain to the kitchen in my cabin and roll the fillet in cornmeal, and fry it, eat it, bite by bite, thinking of my friend Bradley telling me not to do this even if I were starving.

ON MY NEXT TRIP TO TOWN, my third since the attacks, my mother has news for me: she's given Michelle my grandmother's van. I am practically speechless but manage to ask her what changed her mind. "What's the use of holding on to things?" my mother says. "It could all be gone tomorrow. I just hope it helps."

"It will," I say. "Oh, it will."

I call Michelle.

"I know," Michelle says. "I'm two days from being induced, and your mother calls, says she wants to give me the van. She even paid for my first six months of insurance. And license plates."

I think about the two of them, my mother and Michelle, meeting up at the DMV in my hometown to transfer the title and get the license plates changed over. Out of the chaos of 9/11, this small act of kindness.

Aftershocks

That night I make a light dinner—a can of tuna, some crackers—and watch storm clouds gather over Rattlesnake Ridge, heading east. They turn pinkish red in the dusk, then fade to gray. There is lightning but no rain. I've got the AM radio tuned to a station from San Francisco. The Giants are playing baseball, and Barry Bonds is on his way to breaking the home-run record. Between innings there are commercials for local stores, a traffic reporter in a helicopter gives information about crashes and construction delays. The life of the city, just a taste of it, its baseball and traffic, carried on crackling airwaves to my little hideout in the woods some three hundred miles away.

I'd gone to San Francisco once at age nineteen to see the woman whom I would eventually marry and divorce. She was working as a nanny in Palo Alto, and we took a day trip into the city, went down to Fisherman's Wharf, walked back through Chinatown, held hands in Golden Gate Park. Everywhere we went there were homeless people. Legless black Vietnam vets panhandling in their wheelchairs between buildings. The mentally ill stumbling down sidewalks, arguing with themselves. How many more have joined their ranks since then? Can they hear the roar of the crowd tonight as Barry Bonds knocks another hanging curve into McCovey Cove?

After the game, silence seeps back into the cabin—the distant river, the teeming locusts, the soft hiss of propane lamps.

But all the silence in the world can't keep out the bad thoughts.

A few nights later, I'm sitting in the La-Z-Boy recliner reading *Sonny's Blues* by James Baldwin and wondering if I will ever write something as beautiful, sorrowful, and true. As I read along, I begin to smell something. Piercing, acrid, I catch one whiff, then another, and suddenly the stench is everywhere. I drop the book to the floor, pinch my nostrils shut, and look around the cabin, trying to figure out where it's coming from. Finally I open the cabinet under the kitchen sink and pop out a piece of flooring, and there it is: a poisoned mouse, its little gray body beginning to rot. I grab my leather gloves from the breezeway, pull the collar of my T-shirt up over my nose, and peel the dead mouse off the floor. And that's when I see that he is a male. I see the testicles between his tiny back legs.

Long after I've disposed of the body and the smell has cleared out and I've gotten back to reading my book, I see that image. Instead of the words on the page, it's the gray-white fur of the mouse's underbelly. It's the testicles between his little legs. And more than his eyes, ears, nose, and mouth—other parts that we share in common—it's this that breaks my heart.

He was once a tiny mewling baby no bigger than a fingernail. He had a mother and a father who fed and protected him. He was agile, quick, strong, and fierce, perhaps a father himself. And I killed him.

Just like I have killed others before him. Just like the native steelhead I pulled from the river. Just like I was afraid that the men from the fire crew were going to come back and kill me. It has been several days since I've thought of them. Mostly I've tried to put it out of my mind. But tonight, confronted by my own violence, I start thinking about them again. At first I think that if they call, I'll just have to tell them that I'm sorry, I've made a mistake, it's against the rules, and I can't have them over. Then I think that if I tell them such a thing, they'll get pissed off and come anyway. And a bad feeling that I thought had left me suddenly returns: I'm going to be murdered tonight.

I sit with the feeling for as long as I can, trying to read. I know it's the product of too much thinking, too much solitude. Yet I can't seem to make it go away. I look at a sentence on the page, see that dead mouse and his testicles, and know in my bones that they are coming for me. When it gets too bad, when I feel myself shaking, I decide to call my friend Michelle and leave a message.

Aftershocks

Tonight is the night she told me she is to be induced. The baby is overdue. It's time to bring him into the world. I take the satellite phone onto the deck and think about what I want to say.

The phone rings once, then twice, then Michelle picks it up and says hello. I'm surprised to hear her voice and tell her so. She says the hospital got full, they had to reschedule her for later in the week.

"Oh," I say.

"You okay?" she says.

"Let me ask you something."

I tell her I'm afraid I'm going to be murdered tonight and ask if she'll be okay, if my family will be okay, if they'll be able to get over the shock of it. I'm not worried about me, I tell her, I'm worried about the rest of you. And my friend Michelle, two days from giving birth to her first child, responds with perfect calm and clarity. "No one's going to murder you," she says. "Even if they did, we'd be fine."

"You promise?" I say.

"I promise."

After the phone call I feel better for a while. No one's going to come murder me tonight, and even if someone does, my people will cope and get over it. In my journal, I write: *Don't you trust the hearts of those you love? Would you deny them the growth of having to heal from your loss?*

But in bed later that night, in the homestead's deep and utter dark, unable to sleep for all the thoughts scurrying in my mind, I just don't know. Are there wounds that never heal? Even after Jesus told me our divorce hadn't ended my ex-wife's life, the thought of her still hurts me. And even though I can mourn tonight's dead mouse, can imagine him as a mewling baby, can admire the engineering of the nest he made out of threads from my blue jeans and my body hair, it feeds a growing rage. I begin to hate the mouse. His naked tail. His little turds like black sesame seeds on the counter. I want him dead. I want them all dead. Eradicated. Extinct. And then lying in bed, in the dark, the quiet, I hear skittering claws in the kitchen, a mouse dashing across cracked linoleum.

I pop out of bed and grab my miner's headlamp, strap it on. Grab a broom. I'm going to go kill the bastards.

In the kitchen I sit in a chair John Daniel donated to the cabin. It's an office chair on wheels upholstered with Route 66 patches. *Get your kicks on Route 66!* I've got on my miner's headlamp and am scanning the kitchen, the broom across my knees. It's midnight or later. Nothing's moving. I figure the sound of my footsteps must have scared the mice, so I sit still, wait. I train the light away from where they would scurry under the cabinets. In the dark, they will emerge again, thinking they're safe.

A half hour passes. Forty-five minutes. When I look left, I hear skittering on my right. When I look right, I hear skittering on my left. They are playing games with me. Finally I train my light in the middle of the kitchen floor. By watching from the corners of my eyes I can see in both directions.

And I see one.

A smoke-black deer mouse comes walking out of the shadows on his hind feet. Like a human would walk. The mouse doesn't gesture or speak, just looks up at me as though waiting for me to do something. As though daring me to. I'm too taken aback to smash him with my broom, so I just sit there. We watch each other carefully, and after a moment the mouse disappears back into the shadows.

THE NEXT MORNING I WAKE UP and look around the cabin. There is my miner's headlamp on the breakfast table. There is the broom leaning against John Daniel's Route 66 chair. A mess of dishes in the sink. A half-finished letter in the typewriter. I slip out onto the deck and look at Rattlesnake Ridge. The sun is coming up behind it. The Douglas firs cast long shadows down its face. I realize: This is morning. This is the essence of morning. Sunlight dripping like honey into the folds of these craggy mountains. Mist rising from the river. Everything I see is somehow uniquely itself and a part of everything else. The squirrel on the barn roof with a walnut in its mouth. The oxidized garden gate. The sound of a single oak leaf dropping to the forest floor. It was perhaps a moment of understanding like this that motivated John Daniel last winter, during his four months of solitude—in which he made no trips to town, talked to no one—to type out a Zen parable he'd read somewhere and tape it to the cabin wall behind Bradley's old rocking chair:

> A monk introduced himself to the teacher Hsuan-sha, saying, "I have just entered the monastery. Please show me where to enter The Way."
> "Do you hear the sound of the valley stream?" asked Hsuan-sha.
> "Yes," said the monk.
> "Enter there!"

I've been reading this story since I first arrived, and I always thought I understood it. I thought that the master was exposing his young monk's hubris and naïveté by giving him a task that would ultimately prove impossible. Yet this morning, coming to my senses after a night of deep anxiety, gazing out at the rugged Klamath Mountains shrouded in mist and listening to the powerful lapping rapids of the Wild and Scenic Rogue River, I realize that the master is not being glib at all. If anything, he's dead serious. The Way is entered through the sound of the valley stream.

AUTUMN ON

THE ROGUE

WITH THE ARRIVAL OF AUTUMN ON the Rogue and the knowledge that I'll soon be leaving this place, never to return—at least never to return and live in solitude for seven months—even the most ordinary of details are beginning to feel significant: the pulpy yellow insides of a fallen tree a bear has slashed open for grubs; the way light filters through the treetops and makes a banana slug glisten. Like a bear devouring every last morsel in preparation for a long, cold winter, I take my nourishment from what will soon be gone, what I'll remove myself from. I take it on faith that the richness of these days will sustain me in the world I'll return to. For moral support, I have the moon. Since that night early last spring when I first saw it rise like a spaceship over Rattlesnake Ridge—saw it gleaming through the ribs of the tree with the hole in it—I've made a habit of greeting the moon's arrival. October is no different. Only this is the last time I'll see it while here alone. By the end of the month, when the spectacle returns, so will have my father. He and an uncle of mine are set to take a train to Oregon, and the three of us have made plans to drive back to Indiana in my pickup. It will be wonderful to see them, but the moon watching won't be the same. So when the hour draws near, I switch off the propane wall lamps and sit in the rocking chair on the deck. It's cool out, almost chilly, and the night air smells of wood smoke from my stove. As the moon comes up and shoots its wide white beams down the face of Rattlesnake Ridge and out across the meadow, the tangles of blackberries; as it illuminates each shake on the barn roof and the skeletal limbs of the walnut tree; as moonlight turns the river canyon milky blue: I drink it in.

Other days, down at the river, early, the October sunlight bright and cold and fine, I sit on the rocks and contemplate the twisty wisps of steam rising off the water. My mind, like the river, is by turns clear and opaque, shallow and deep. Thoughts recklessly plunge ahead over big boulders only to eddy around on themselves at a tangle of roots, as though reconsidering. I sit until my legs tingle and my hands feel weightless, and when I'm tired of sitting I take up my fly rod. For me, this is the real meditation: sending a fly skimming through the air to land in the water without so much as a splash—the way an insect would land. It's a relinquishment of all distractions, a paring down to the essential. From an open, fishy-looking spot clear of willows, I drop my orange fly into the current, let out a good amount of fly line, and lift my rod tip past my shoulder to one o'clock, whipping the line back behind me. Then I snap my wrist forward, angling the rod to eleven o'clock. Because it is heavy, the line shoots out ahead of the fly and lies down on the water like an uncurling breaker, and the fly (if I have done everything right) settles on the far side of the river, as though hovering on iridescent wings.

Autumn on the Rogue

I don't get every cast exactly right, and even perfect casts don't always yield a fish, but time and again it happens: that flash of silver, my rod doubling over. Sometimes I take the fish up to the cabin, fry them for lunch, and savor the flaky pink morsels of their flesh, the crispy bits of skin. More often, however, I'm content to land them and for a moment hold their flopping weight in my hands.

But no matter how long I sit by the river or how long I fish, no matter how many fish I hold in my hands: the morning gives way to afternoon, the afternoon gives way to evening. The days fall away from me.

In October, just as in the spring—when the temperatures are comfortable and the fishing is good—there is a spike in visitors to the homestead. Several weekends in a row Bradley makes the trip down from Portland to go fishing. We hit every hole along our stretch of river, and every hole, I learn, has a story: Mom's Rock, Dad's Rock, Francis Creek, Copsey Creek. Between casts Bradley tells me that this is where a bear got after his mother. This is where his father always fished. We pause to watch water ouzels flit among the rapids. We pick at a salmon carcass washed up on the rocks, examine its bones. It comes to me that this must be one of the reasons Bradley takes such an active hand in sponsoring the writing residency: it's a chance to share his life and stories with people who love this place as much as he does.

"What am I going to do," I ask Bradley one day, "when I can't just come down here and see this anymore?"

We have fished our way a few miles upstream and are sitting on "the hump," a big mound overlooking the river. All around us are chiseled rocks, lichens, wild grapevines scaling the yellow-leafed river oaks. I have been telling him that even though I love it out here in Oregon, I need to go home to Indiana. That Indiana has a beauty and a wildness all its own, just nothing quite like this.

"It's your funeral," Bradley laughs.

"I know."

"There's beauty everywhere," he says, nodding, considering. "But me? I couldn't do it. Couldn't leave this behind." I tell him I know he's right, but it's where I want to be. "It's your funeral," he says again.

As we fish along, I try to imagine the life in which I don't go back to Indiana but instead stay here, stay close to the Rogue. Maybe I could move to Grants Pass, teach at a community college, and keep writing my stories, maybe someday publish a book. But there is the question of my rapidly dwindling bank account, my truck payment, the effort of moving across the country. All things that could be done if I wanted to badly enough, if I put in the work, made the sacrifice—and a small voice inside is saying yes, you'd be a fool to go home. More profound than that voice, however, is my desire to see home with fresh eyes, to return with the insights afforded me by this half-year alone. Someday I'll be called off again, on another journey. For now I feel called home.

MID-OCTOBER BRINGS THE FIRST RAINS since May, soft and drizzly, and the rains bring deer—females emerging from their hiding places, males out on the prowl. And all this deer activity brings road hunters. On my weekly trips to town, I see their rigs parked alongside ditches and turnouts. Rusty Toyotas. Jeeps. Sometimes I see the hunters themselves, dressed in camouflage pants and jackets, skinning a buck in the misting rain. Sometimes we pull up window to window and have a conversation.

"Where's the meat?" one man jovially shouts at me. On the cluttered dashboard of his truck rests a rifle.

"Don't know," I tell him.

He's middle-aged, fat, sandy-haired, wearing a red felt fedora pushed back on his head. He wants to know if I'm out hunting, and when I say no, he scrunches up his face, asks why the hell not, and laughs like crazy.

Autumn on the Rogue

Only after a few of these encounters do I put together what's going on: these men and their buddies get liquored up, grab their rifles and deer tags, hop in their pickups, and troll these back-country logging roads for deer. It's not exactly sporting—and I can only guess as to its legality—but I imagine that for these guys road hunting must beat the hell out of sitting in some deer stand, cold and bored, no one to talk to, nothing to do but wait. And I start to understand what it means to them to meet me on the road like this. It's like racing ten miles down a lake at the break of dawn only to find another boat anchored in your favorite fishing spot. That I'm not even hunting—that I've driven through and scared off all the deer and am not even hunting—beats all.

Not that every road hunter matches this description. One day I meet an old man in a blue Jeep. He's got the same hat as the others, the same camouflage vest, the same deer rifle lying across the dash. But he's by himself and not so much road hunting as he is just driving around, looking out at the mountains. His skin is paper thin, with liver spots all over his hands, and under the red hat is hair so white it's almost blue, like bone china. If this old man bagged a deer, what would he do with it?

We pull up window to window, and I introduce myself, explain my presence back here, and he nods, takes it in, then starts telling stories from years back with references to people and places I've never heard of before. He looks out at the mountains, wistfully, seeing everything he says come back to life.

"Used to call this Peacock Hill," he says, nodding. "A buddy and me, we'd say, 'Let's try up on Peacock Hill.'"

When I ask him why they called it Peacock Hill, he laughs and says that one year they saw a big peacock strutting up the road. "Full plumage and everything," he says. "But we never told nobody. Not a soul."

"Why not?"

He licks his lips, thinks about it a second, and grins with a full set of square white teeth the same bone-china blue as his hair. He says, "Hell, with our luck it would've been some kind of endangered peacock, and they'd have had scientists and environmentalists up here so fast. They'd have shut the whole place down. We were almost sorry we didn't shoot the damn thing. To be over and done with it!"

With all the traffic on these backcountry logging roads lately, I half expect to run into the guys from the fire squad downriver. Though they have the number to my satellite phone and I keep expecting them to call, they haven't called. They don't call. And at some point I realize that they aren't going to call, that I have somehow dodged a bullet. Maybe they lost the number. Maybe they weren't serious about coming back in the first place. Regardless, I feel lucky and grateful I don't have to admit my mistake to Bradley. Though I am disappointed with myself for allowing the situation to develop as far as it did, the thought of ever disappointing Bradley, who has so freely shared his love of the homestead with me, would feel a hundred times worse. So just as the old road hunter who saw the peacock up in these hills has his secret to keep, I have mine.

ANOTHER OF THE OCTOBER VISITORS is Dave Reed. He and a buddy from the BLM come to do some survey work at the river, the gist of which—even though I tag along—I never quite understand. They are surveying ten-by-ten plots of land all down the river, creating a checkerboard-shaped grid, and attempting to catalog the various trees and plants. Dave's friend has a little notebook into which he jots all kinds of information. When he's finished writing, he pulls out a digital camera and takes pictures of the plot. The camera has a recording device, and he pushes a button, narrates a quick, functional caption: "This is plot XX. October 19th, 2001. Rogue River. Facing south."

I bring my fly rod with me on the hike, and when the shadow of the western cliffs crosses the water, I take off to fish.

I promise Dave and his coworker steelhead for dinner and want to impress them with my prowess as a fisherman. As a writer and a student of stories, however, I should know better than to promise. Up and down the river, plying waters that in days past have produced unyielding numbers of fish, I catch nothing. Not even a nibble. At dusk, I meet up with Dave and his friend empty-handed.

Fortunately, they've brought plenty of food—cheese and crackers and the season's last ripe tomatoes from someone's home garden. We stay up late drinking beer, telling stories, watching the stars come out, and, all in all, it's a pleasant visit and I enjoy their company. The next morning, however, two things happen that hurt me. The first is that Dave, having learned that yellowjackets have made a nest at the base of the cabin, sets out to solve the problem. Early in the morning, the air still chilly and cool, he fetches a can of Bee-Bomb from his truck, stands back about ten feet, and shoots the insecticide concoction—a long wet string of it—into the open mouth of the hive. A few black yellowjackets crawl out, gasping, and die in the dirt. The rest are asphyxiated in the hive. I watch helplessly, thinking that, yes, it wouldn't do anyone any good for yellowjackets to start stinging the cabin's occupant or his guests; and thinking, yes, if a bear got interested in eating the yellowjackets, he could tear hell out of the cabin to get after them (because I've already seen bear damage to a tool shed across from the upper house, where one clawed through five-eighths-inch-thick plywood as though through honeycomb); but also thinking of all the mornings I've sat quietly on the deck, watching one yellowjacket after another spark toward the garden, their hollow bodies filling with sunlight.

The second thing isn't as much of an event as it is a confirmation of something I already suspect. When Dave is finished with the Bee-Bomb I walk him up the road and point out the bald cypress that Ian Boyden planted in honor of his grandfather.

During the time I was freaking out after 9/11, I had neglected the tree and its watering needs. Now several of its outer needles are turning rust-orange.

I ask Dave if it looks salvageable.

"Oh, it's dead," Dave says.

Part of what makes this news difficult is that the tree is dead because I failed to take care of it. The other part that makes this difficult is that two days after Dave Reed's visit, Bradley brings his mother down to the homestead. After a life of coming here—first to a mining claim at Horseshoe Bend, then later to the homestead itself—she now visits just once a year in October. Bradley and John Daniel and Joe Green have told me how wonderful she is, how full of stories, and all summer I have been looking forward to meeting her. I have been looking forward to showing her the tree Ian planted in honor of her late husband. The tree it now appears that I have killed.

This same weekend brings John Daniel, on Friday afternoon. He's writing a book about his winter hiatus. He talked to no one—no one—for four and a half months. He's here to reconnect, if briefly, with the silence of the river canyon and the river itself, and to compose an article *Audubon* has asked him to write. The prompt: after 9/11 why does nature still matter?

We spend the afternoon fishing, I with my fly rod and John with a spinning rod at the end of which is a gleaming stainless-steel spoon. Neither of us manages to catch a fish—they just won't bite. We talk about why nature still matters after 9/11, agree that the question suggests part of the problem.

How we see 9/11.

How do the terrible and shocking losses of this one day compare to losses that go on every day but are rendered invisible by virtue of who they happen to—the poor and oppressed, who have no voice? And if tragedies and staggering injustices are commonplace, then the question after 9/11 isn't why nature still matters. It's the ones Thoreau formulated after climbing Mount Katahdin: *Who* are we? *Where* are we? Who are we that we should do these things to one another? Where are we that dogmatic fantasies of an otherworldly Heaven or Paradise take precedence over the solid Earth?

The night of Margery and Bradley's arrival at the homestead whiskey is poured over ice, and Bradley barbecues chunks of a thirty-pound salmon Margery hauled out of the Salmon River up near Otis, Oregon, a few days before. For an appetizer we have the salmon's roe with crackers. Margery learned the technique for making caviar from her son Frank, who learned it from a Japanese woman. You dip the skeins of eggs into boiling water for three seconds, then use your fingers and slide the eggs into a pot of cold water. Skim off what rises to the top, then rinse repeatedly, drain, and fold in a pinch of salt (not iodized). The eggs turn from milky peach to orange.

These little orange eggs, gelatinous, salty—I put a small scoop in my mouth and break them apart with my tongue. They coat the back of my throat with salty river water. "The taste of life," John says.

At eighty-nine Margery's hair has gone white, and there are wrinkles on her face, faint liver spots on her wrists. In her eyes, however, is the glow of youth, remembering. As the night deepens and we start dinner, she tells stories about the hermits she knew along the river, about alcoholic jet-boat drivers and bush pilots. My favorite story is about a woman who lived with her husband in a hand-hewn shack along the river. The fishing guides would take their "dudes" down to this woman's cabin to show off the local color, and the "dudes" would inevitably make a nuisance of themselves, opening drawers, looking in closets. One day the woman asks a man where he lives. "Akron, Ohio," he said.

"What street?" she said.

"Why?"

"I want to look in your closets."

Another night they all got to drinking, and for some reason or other she got mad at her husband, pulled out a revolver, and shot him. In the arm. "But the husband wouldn't press charges down in Gold Beach," Margery laughs. "He didn't know where else he'd find a woman who would chop him his firewood."

A Chinook salmon barbecued just right, a good Kentucky bourbon courtesy of John Daniel, a sky full of stars. By the end of the night I am in full appreciation of the gift that has worked in my life to bring me to this moment, to the flickering light on all of their faces: John, Bradley, Margery. We talk about black bears, about the fight of halfpounder steelhead. Margery with her little glass of whiskey tells about how before the river was dammed it used to flood every spring, and that when the river flooded, its roar—so ever present in the canyon—went silent, that the floods drowned out the rapids, and the quiet here deepened. On the quarter-mile hike back to my cabin at midnight, in the dark, alone, having left behind the warmth and light and companionship of the upper house, my heart surges with gratitude. The feeling is so strong that when I hear a thrashing in the forest not far from me—the sound of several black-tailed deer snorting their alarm calls and bounding stiff-legged through the bracken—I am not in the least afraid.

BEFORE HEADING HOME THE NEXT AFTERNOON, Bradley drives Margery down to the lower house so she can take a look at the garden. In her day, Margery was a master gardener. Peppers and tomatoes, cucumbers, squash, you name it, and she grew it. She and Bradley's father even used to make homemade wine from the grapes. I had planned on having a big garden myself, but I hadn't been prepared for (and hadn't understood) just how dry it gets in the summer. My garden got fried.

"Did you have tomatoes?" Margery asks.

Autumn on the Rogue

"No." I shake my head.

She nods thoughtfully, looks around, says this was a great year for tomatoes, but there was no way I could have known. We stand in the shade of the apple trees. I tell her the apples did well, the Concord grapes.

I show her the butterfly bush Ian and Jenny planted, then the apricot tree, the pear tree. After looking around at the garden a while, we head up the road, and I show her the bald cypress I have killed. Every needle has gone to rust. Dave Reed had laughed when I asked if it were at all salvageable. Margery, on the other hand, just looks at the tree, studies it a second. She asks if she has heard correctly, if it's a *bald* cypress. I confirm the name and tell her what Ian had told me: that it can live to be more than four thousand years old, that it is revered in Japan. And I confess that it's probably my fault the tree died, that I hadn't realized how much water everything here needed.

"Well, if it's called a *bald* cypress," Margery says, "maybe that just means it drops its needles in the fall."

When it's time for them all to go—John Daniel, Bradley, Margery—they leave me with a bottle of red wine and some homemade smoked salmon. A front is moving in, and the air has gone cool and windy. The sky is gray over Rattlesnake Ridge. I sit on the deck, thinking about the recent flurry of activity: the road hunters out looking for deer, Dave Reed and his coworker from the BLM doing their surveys, my fishing trips with Bradley and John, and Margery's stories of years gone by on the river. And I think about what's ahead. In two weeks I'll meet my father and an uncle at the bus station in Eugene, and after a few nights here at the homestead we will get in the truck and head south to California, east across Nevada, Utah, and Wyoming. We'll pass through Nebraska, Iowa, and Illinois, and arrive finally in Indiana. I think about the miles to come, think about the friends and family waiting for me at the end of the line. How good it will feel to see them all. In the meantime, Bradley has given me a list of chores for getting the homestead prepped for the winter—change the oil in the mower, defrost the freezer, and so forth. A few chores, then some fishing and hiking. I'll read a book, write a few last letters home, spend some quality time just staring into the fire in the stove, holding my hands up to it for warmth. And all the while I will know: even though I had given it up for dead, the bald cypress Ian planted in honor of his late grandfather is, in fact, alive.

On my last day at the homestead alone a fine softly falling mist slicks the yellow leaves of the walnut tree by the barn, blackens its trunk. After breakfast I haul in a few armloads of firewood and start a fire in the stove. The smell of rain mixes with the burning newspaper I've rolled for kindling. Plumes of smoke drift from the chimney into the garden, hang like fog over the grass. After a dusty and sun-bleached summer, a summer of heat, silence, and solitary communion with the homestead, the colors brought out by the rain astonish me. The brown of the barn's cedar shakes. The driveway's brick red. The deep-green, almost blue, needles of the Douglas firs. Even Cougar-Bait and friends get into the act, their snouts turning white with the rut. I watch them on their morning excursion to the salt block. Rain darkens their frayed summer coats. Their antlers shine. One cranes his neck, lifts a long hind leg, and scratches behind his ear.

I am feeling very good today: I'm dry and warm, listening to the sound of rain on the roof, logs crackling in the stove. I'm reminded of a school day from first or second grade. A gentle thunderstorm swept through town, and all morning I kept looking out the window at the wet grass and the puddles, the little splash made by each raindrop in the asphalt parking lot. I loved the rain, and I knew I loved the rain. I knew I was sitting in my classroom, looking outside and loving the rain.

Autumn on the Rogue

What I know this morning is that my time here is ending, that tomorrow I'll pick up my father and my uncle and we'll soon head home. Like the rain, this thought makes everything shine. Even my loneliness.

I love my loneliness.

Yesterday I saw a mother bear and her two cubs. They were scurrying along the edge of the forest, their black coats catching the last bit of sunlight, and I wanted nothing more than to dig a den on one of these wild mountainsides, hunker down, and ride out the winter with them. An impossibility I nevertheless have to mourn. Just as I have to mourn the bears I've been hearing at night lately, as I lie in bed. They're up in the old orchard below the upper house, thrashing the unfenced apple trees, making apples rain down in an attempt to put on as much winter weight as possible. Their lives here go on, even as I'm leaving. My consolation is that their lives here go on.

Midmorning I tamp down the little fire in my stove, grab my fly rod and my pack, and slip out into the mist. Down at the river, at the beach where Ogden and his rafting party camped for the night, a month's worth of wind and now this light rain have erased their tracks. I climb the rock from which the boys cannonballed into the river and look around: to the east, the river is wide, calm, meandering over a series of shallow, sparkling gravel bars; to the west, the river narrows, plunges through a gauntlet of huge boulders, and creates the rapids I hear at the homestead, the soft and ever-present sound of the valley stream. I head that direction. The rocks are slick with the morning rain and the mist off the rapids—slick, black, and jagged. A fall would hurt. So I move slowly, carefully, looking down from time to time into the deep white-water surges, feeling their reverberations in my stomach, my sternum, the palms of my hands. Thousands of gallons of water a second. Every second of every day. Metamorphic rock so hard it holds its shape and in turn gives shape to the river. And contained within these forces, like DNA, like spirit, the ephemeral colors made by this play of water and light stake their claim on who and where I am. The deep glassy green of the river. The slick black rocks. The rainbow hovering in the misting white water like the rainbow down the side of a steelhead.

Autumn on the Rogue

EPILOGUE

Since I haven't been working half the year and my bank account is nearly empty, I spend November, December, and the first few weeks of January in my parents' basement. They live on the edge of a small town, on ten acres of creek bottom, which includes a farm pond. In the drizzly winter cold I take walks down there. It's a quiet and nice place to walk, but it isn't wilderness. I hear cars and semitrailers zooming up 1-65 a few miles to our east. The neighbors' dogs bark at all hours. When I climb up the hill to the house hoping for the good burn in the lungs that the trail home from the Rogue used to give me, I find I'm not even breathing hard. To manage, I try to remind myself of the aphorism I read in a book about Chinese hermits: "The little hermit lives in the forest; the big hermit lives in the city." Only very slowly and with much effort do I begin to accept that a return to civilization requires every bit the adjustment of a departure, and that my work now is to cultivate solitude in the midst of other people.

In mid-January I string a few jobs together and raise enough capital to move into an apartment in a drafty old Victorian home in Lafayette. The neighbors across the hall are heavy smokers, so I keep the windows cracked and sleep at night in a sleeping bag rated for comfort at fifteen degrees. In the apartment below me lives the local TV weatherman, Buzz Lopez. Whenever anyone sees him, they complain about the cold. He says he'll see what he can do. My problem isn't with the weather or the smokers—it's the squirrels that have taken up residency in the rotten gutters outside my window. They scratch like rats, and, at night, I hear them mating.

For work I have three part-time jobs. I teach an Introduction to Composition class at Purdue. I tutor graduate students from China who must pass a test that certifies them as proficient English speakers so they may keep their teaching assistantships and stay in the United States. Then on Monday, Tuesday, and Wednesday nights (with a Saturday shift from eight until noon) I work at the YWCA. I am the basketball guy for a youth league. I get out the balls, make sure the gym is ready, pick up trash left in the bleachers by thoughtless parents. On Saturdays, during the games, I sell popcorn and candy.

All in all, it's not a terrible life. When I'm not working I go for walks downtown and peer into empty shops and boarded-up buildings, wondering about all the lives that ran their courses here. I go to the library at Purdue and wander the stacks. I hit a coffee shop and drink strong coffee, people-watch, read about shamanism and circumpolar bear cults. Sometimes, afterward, out on the street, I just stare at the traffic, watching the flow of headlights as though watching a river, mesmerized by the revving engines and the steaming exhaust from tailpipes and the faint splashes of music that wash over me like waves as the cars pass by. Some friends are concerned and think I've gone a little kooky in the head, and maybe I have. Maybe it's a good thing. Not much has changed around here: same grid of streets and buildings, same sights and smells. Were it not for the small differences—friends who have altered their hairstyles, who have gotten new glasses, who have broken up with one romantic partner and started dating another—I might be inclined to think of my time in Oregon as one long and languid dream. There are nights when I'll be playing chess with Big Aaron, or watching Michelle's baby boy so she can lie down for an hour or two, when I will think about how I had been living out there and feel astonished, as though I don't know that person. Was that really me chasing a bear with a weed eater? Trying to hand-feed apples to a deer? Did I sleep with a gun in my bed because I was convinced—*convinced*—I was going to be murdered?

One bit of proof that my time in Oregon isn't a dream is that, unlike everyone else I know, I haven't seen the television footage from 9/11. I have seen photographs, and for days I sat and listened to coverage on the radio, but I haven't seen the film of the planes smashing one and then another into the World Trade Center. My mother taped some of the footage, thinking I would want to watch it when I returned from the homestead. As grateful as I am to my mother for thinking of me, however, I don't want to watch the murder of three thousand people. Because of this, my family discounts my opposition to the mounting calls for war with Iraq. One night over dinner, it comes to a head when my father says someone's forgetting about 9/11. Then my mother says someone hasn't seen the footage. My brother says someone's afraid to watch it.

In the seven months I spent in the backcountry, in relative solitude, I rarely felt as alone as I do sitting at this table.

Later in the spring things get a little better. I make friends with a woman in the creative writing program, a poet named Rebecca. She is originally from Massachusetts but before moving to Indiana had been living in Southern California, where she went to college. The Midwest is a change of pace for her, and she describes to me with something like horror her first trip to a Super Wal-Mart.

So I try to show her some of Indiana's better features. We drive north of town and take pictures of horses in a March snowstorm. We go out to dinner at hole-in-the-wall restaurants. It feels good to make a new friend, someone who didn't know me before. There is less to explain somehow. One day at a coffee shop in Lafayette, I show her my pictures from the homestead. The lower house, the barn, a view of the mountains from out on the deck. I try to point out the tree with the hole in it, but it's too small to see. She looks at each picture in turn and listens to my stories.

The other good development this spring is a financial one. My late grandmother's estate has been settled, and I inherit five thousand dollars. With the YWCA youth league finishing up in April and the end of the academic year fast approaching, the money couldn't come at a better time. Together with what I've managed to save (I'm the definition of frugal), part of the money will go to subsidizing this summer's writing. I've got an idea for a novel, and with two and a half months until the fall semester begins, I can make great progress. Maybe I will even revise the short stories I wrote at the homestead with an eye toward putting together a collection. With the other part of the money, I buy an expensive pair of hiking boots and a plane ticket to Portland, Oregon. Powered by nostalgia, Joe Green, his wife, Marquita, and I have decided to hike the Rogue River Trail.

This is something I have been dreaming about in my drafty apartment all spring—seeing that glassy green water again, watching osprey swoop up and down the canyon with gasping steelhead in their talons, sleeping out under the stars. The Rogue River

Trail is forty miles long, and we set aside four days for hiking, with one extra night to be spent at the homestead. This year's writer-resident is a young poet from Montana named Henrietta Goodman, who has brought to the homestead her dog and her three-year-old son, Cole. I look forward to meeting her and hearing about how solitude has treated her so far. I look forward to seeing the lower house, the barn, the garden. Will Cougar-Bait and his friends be around? Will they remember me? I haven't gotten over leaving the homestead—that much is clear. Whether the trip back will mitigate my feelings or merely exacerbate them remains to be seen. "It's your funeral," Bradley laughed last fall on one of our fishing trips, when I told him I had to go home. He was joking around, but there was a grain of truth in what he said. That person alone at the homestead lived what at times felt like a heroic existence, one with boundless riches. He now makes a living by teaching Introduction to Composition and fetching basketballs for kids at the YWCA.

But I have my secrets. Because I am comfortable with silence and do not speak out of an anxiety to be heard, I am better able to listen to the students in my classes and ask them the right kinds of questions. Because I went so long without human contact, my smile is genuine when I make change for people buying candy bars those Saturday mornings at the Y. None of them know, and none of them needs to know, what I have seen in the wilderness. I now live the peace I felt out there.

This is not to say I have achieved some kind of enlightenment, because I haven't. I still get angry, frustrated, sad. I still wonder if I haven't made a mistake in coming back to Indiana after a stint in the West.

What's changed for me after living at the homestead—the real secret I possess—is that there is room in my heart for all these feelings. I am not beholden to fear or self-pity. Inside me there is a wilderness river I can sit beside all morning, a mountain range receding into the dusk, a sky full of stars.

On the first day of our trip, Joe, Marquita, and I leave our car behind at the Grave Creek Bridge, having paid someone to drive it to Foster Bar, where the trail ends. We hike six and a half hilly miles with forty-pound backpacks, set up our tent at Slate Slide campsite, and, after a quick dinner of rehydrated chicken and Ramen noodles, wander off in our separate directions. Marquita, a talented artist, has found a bone shard—what looks like a broken piece of deer femur—and sits sketching it. Down at water's edge, Joe has taken off his hiking boots and socks and is sitting in the sand, writing in a notebook. I've brought a notebook, too, but don't feel like writing. Instead I climb onto a boulder and sit with my arms circling my knees, watching the sun go down in the West. Another day and we'll hit the homestead, meet the new caretaker. "What a gift!" I can hear Bradley saying. The sound of the river, the sun going down, Joe, Marquita, the soreness in my shoulders from carrying a pack. What a gift. This day and the next.

Epilogue